the scrapbook designer's workbook

by kari hansen

MEMORY MAKERS BOOKS
Cincinnati, Ohio

www.memorymakersmagazine.com

11 10 09 08 07 5 4 3 2 1

Distributed in Canada by Fraser Direct
100 Armstrong Avenue
Georgetown, ON, Canada L7G 5S4
Tel: (905) 877-4411

Distributed in the U.K. and Europe by David & Charles
Brunel House, Newton Abbot, Devon, TQ12 4PU, England
Tel: (+44) 1626 323200, Fax: (+44) 1626 323319
Email: postmaster@davidandcharles.co.uk

Distributed in Australia by Capricorn Link
P.O. Box 704, S. Windsor NSW, 2756 Australia
Tel: (02) 4577-3555

Library of Congress Cataloging-in-Publication Data
Hansen, Kari
  The scrapbook designer's workbook : unlocking the secrets to great page design / Kari Hansen.
     p. cm.
  Includes index.
  ISBN-13: 978-1-892127-95-2 (hardcover, concealed wire-o : alk. paper)
  ISBN-10: 1-892127-95-4 (hardcover, concealed wire-o : alk. paper)
  1. Photograph albums. 2. Photographs--Conservation and restoration.
3. Scrapbooks. I. Title.
TR501.H36 2006
745.593--dc22
                              2006027952

Editor: Lydia Rueger
Designer: Melanie Warner
Production Coordinator: Matt Wagner
Photographers: Tim Grondin, Al Parrish

Memory Makers Books is the home of *Memory Makers*, the scrapbook magazine dedicated to educating and inspiring scrapbookers. To subscribe, or for more information, call (800) 366-6465.
Visit us on the Internet at **www.memorymakersmagazine.com**

Supplies: Pink, ivory cardstocks · Patterned papers (Anna Griffin) · Covered button kit (Prym-Dritz) · Thread · Gingham fabric · Ribbon · Thread

dedication

For my parents, Connie and Tracy Hansen
for teaching me that I could be anything
I dreamed of when I grew up

For my husband, Tom Daffin
for giving me the freedom to be
an artist when I grew up

acknowledgments

My thanks to the Denver staff of *Memory Makers* magazine for their support and faith in me while I worked on the Designer's Workbook column. In particular, hugs to Shawna Rendon.

My thanks to my book editor, Lydia Rueger, and the Memory Makers Books staffs in Denver and Cincinnati for working with me to bring this project to life.

Last but not least, my overflowing gratitude goes to my fellow scrapbook artists. I am constantly inspired by your passion and creativity. This book would not exist without you!

contents

14 Introduction to Design

30 Elements of Design

56 Color

90 Principles of Design

A few fun and funky random facts about me:

I published my own magazine when I was ten years old. It was called the Crazy about Cats Newsletter.

My father made up the spelling up my name when I was born, in part because he thought K was a particularly nice letter. I'm glad he did!

My husband Tom and I have been married for five years, but we have known each other for nineteen.

I think the world's problems could be solved if FlyLady, super-Nanny and Oprah were in charge.

I don't just wear shoes, I collect them! But forget the Manolos for me; I prefer Doc Martens and Fluevogs.

K factor

My most significant factors

Supplies: Black, pink cardstocks · Patterned papers (Anna Griffin) · Rose building stamp (Stamp A Mania) · Deckle edge scissors (Fiskars) · Fabric · Covered button kit (Prym-Dritz) · Ribbon · Heart pins (Heidi Grace) · Corner rounder (EK Success) · Thread · Foam adhesive (3L) · ClassizismAntiqua font · Charlesworth font

Large photo: Michelle Pesce, Foxfish Photography

meet the author

In a 2002 meeting to discuss potential new columns for the upcoming year, the editorial staff of *Memory Makers* magazine, on which I was the craft editor, talked about how the needs of our readers had changed over the years. As scrapbookers had become more savvy and their pages more sophisticated, they had begun to seek out more in-depth knowledge about the concepts behind their pages. Rather than being content to copy layouts from magazines and idea books, they wanted to understand why certain designs were appealing in the first place. Scrapbookers were becoming increasingly aware of design, and by doing so, were seeking to become designers themselves. We concluded that a section dedicated to teaching design theory could be a welcome addition to the magazine, and the Designer's Workbook column was born.

When Executive Editor Debbie Mock suggested that I helm the new series, I was honored to accept. For the next two years, the column tackled an aspect of design in each issue. In the course of researching and writing each piece, I was able to revisit with a new perspective the lessons learned during my art school days. Adapting basic design concepts to apply to the scrapbooking medium was an amazing learning experience for me. Not only did I have the chance to share design with others, but I grew as an artist in the process. It has been my privilege to share the beauty of design with my fellow scrapbook artists.

I am thrilled to now compile the Designer's Workbook column into a book. In addition to gathering each install-ment into one easy-to-reference format, creating this book has given me the opportunity to expand on the information and artwork from the original series. Each section show-cases specific elements and principles of design on layouts, tags and cards. There are also charts and helpful hints to help you develop your skills. Design terms are collected into a glossary at the back of the book for your reference.

Whether you previously read the magazine column or this is your first glimpse of Designer's Workbook, I hope this book will inspire you, teach you a design foundation, and help you grow into the scrapbook artist you aspire to be.

Best wishes on your creative journey!

Kari

Kari Hansen, author and artist

in the studio

Welcome to my studio! Pour yourself a cup of coffee, pull up a chair, and let's talk about scrapbooking design. If I could have you over to crop with me in my home studio, I certainly would. (I know we would have a great time!) But since that isn't possible, the next best thing is a photo tour of my creative space. I want you feel as if, in reading this book, you are stepping into my studio and learning design with me. So, in addition to showing you around so you can see where I work, we'll begin with a question-and-answer session between my editor, Lydia Rueger, and me so you can get to know me and my design philosophies a little better. Come on in, make yourself at home and get ready to explore the elements of design.

A dining table with an indestructible granite top gives me lots of room to spread out and work on pages.

Photo: Michelle Pesce, Foxfish Photography

artist Q&A

Q When did you start scrapbooking?

A I have enjoyed rubber stamping and paper crafts since I was a teenager, but was resistant to scrapbooking at first. This was partly because I didn't think I fit into the craft's demographic and partly because of the stereotype of how layouts were supposed to look. While visiting family during the 2001 Christmas holidays, I tried it for the first time with my mum and sister, who had been scrapbooking for several years. A few months later, I was making pages on my own, and it didn't take long before I was completely hooked! The time was ideal for me to take a second look at the hobby, as it was starting to grow and become a more sophisticated art form.

Q When did you know you wanted to be an artist?

A I don't think there was ever a point when I made a conscious decision to become an artist; I just always was one. There were always music, crafts, books and games around when I was a child, and my father consistently pursued creative outlets. I was encouraged to express myself in that manner and to use my imagination.

When making plans for college, I chose to study art history in addition to studio arts so I could learn about all types of art, and get a formal foundation to build on the creativity of my childhood.

Q How would you describe your scrapbook style?

A My layouts have a linear foundation with layers of detail and texture. Color, mixing patterns and typography particularly interest me. While I am interested in digital techniques, I think I will always be a "traditional" scrapbook artist because I am drawn to the tactile quality of the craft. I like to figure out how to make things myself, so I am more likely to use a homemade embellishment than a store-bought piece. I enjoy the process as much as the finished result, so I am definitely not a fast, page-in-an-hour kind of scrapbook artist! Also, I believe that journaling is an important aspect of a layout and should be included most of the time, even though it can be the hardest part.

Q What artist(s) have influenced you and why?

A A favorite is Charles Rennie Mackintosh, a Scottish architect and designer in the Art Nouveau style. I am drawn to the stylized organic linearity and the balance of feminine and masculine in his work. I also like Frank Lloyd Wright and William Morris, who integrated exterior design with interior decorative arts in order to create entire visual environments. From the fine arts category, a few of my favorites are John Singer Sargent, Henri Matisse, Marc Chagall and Carl Larsson. While each has quite a different approach, they are all colorists with extraordinary eyes for detail and composition.

Each drawer of this blueprint-style cabinet holds a different category of stamps, from animals to botanicals.

Photo: Michelle Pesce, Foxfish Photography

Q What is your favorite part of your home studio?

A I bought a dining table with an indestructible granite top at a discount furniture store, so I have lots of room to spread out when I work. One of the coolest things in my studio is the rubber stamp case my father built for me, inspired by a blueprint cabinet. The family room in our basement is shared between my studio and my husband's home office (with his multiple computers), and I love that we can be in the same space even while working on individual projects.

Q What do you listen to while you are creating?

A My iPod is essential when I work, with a play-list that ranges from James Taylor to Nine Inch Nails, the B-52s to the Smiths, Death Cab for Cutie to the Pixies. If I want high energy I lean toward industrial music, but I am just as likely to mellow out with Keane or Coldplay. It just depends on my mood. I also like to listen to audio books while I work, and enjoy mysteries and science fiction/fantasy books. Audio books allow me to indulge in literature, while keeping my hands free to create.

Q What is your best organizational tip?

A My best advice is to organize your supplies in a way that complements the way you work. It works well for me to organize items by either category or color. For example, I separate lettering products by material such as metal, wood or plastic. Items such as ribbon, buttons and paper are divided by color since that is how I look for those pieces as I design. I throw away most of the packaging that products come in because that takes up a lot of space. I use zippered baggies within my bins and drawers to keep like items together.

Q What supply do you tend to use the most?

A I have an insane amount of patterned paper, and regularly mix patterns on my layouts. It seems I can hardly make a page without using ribbon, buttons and foam adhesive. I love to collect and use rubber stamps. I also have thousands of computer fonts, and choosing just the right ones for a project is an important part of the design process for me. In general, I just like stuff! I am a collector and hoarder of tactile bits that might just be perfect for a future project. So, while I aspire to declutter the rest of my house, I don't try to reign in my pack rat tendencies when it comes to my studio! Instead, I just try to keep it organized and accessible.

Q What are you doing currently to challenge yourself as an artist?

A As a designer, I am challenging myself to think outside the box and approach composition in fresh ways. I have also been working on designing tight, integrated units within layout compositions and approaching typography in unique ways. Over the next year, I aspire to broaden my knowledge of photography and digital techniques through reading, taking classes and experimenting.

Ribbons and papers are sorted by color and placed in clear storage containers for easy access.

Photo: Michelle Pesce, Foxfish Photography

take an artist's field trip

To help inspire fresh ideas while working on this book, I took an artist's field trip to the Great American Quilt Factory in Denver.

Field trips are not just for school kids! They are also wonderful opportunities for your inner artist. In *The Artist's Way*, Julie Cameron encourages artists to "fill the well" of their creativity by setting aside time each week to embark on some kind of stimulating visual activity. The intention of an artist's field trip is to take in new textures, color combinations, patterns, materials and anything else that will spark your creativity and inspire a fresh perspective. Make a date with your inner artist and pencil this personal time into your calendar. Plan to go on your own so you have no distractions and can focus on exploring your destination. Take a notebook to jot down ideas and sketch designs. You don't have to spend a cent on a field trip; just stroll around and take everything in.

field trip destinations

* fabric and quilting stores
* hardware store
* art supply store
* any photogenic place you might find for a picture-taking excursion
* bookstore
* art museum
* art collective shop
* stationery store
* library
* party supply store
* another artist's studio
* workshop or class at an art supply store or community college
* nature center
* clothing store (I especially love Anthropologie, Oilily and Urban Outfitters)
* scrapbook and craft stores (of course!)

Photos: Michelle Pesce, Foxfish Photography

keep an inspiration journal

Since you never know when an inspirational idea will strike or how fast you may forget it, keep a journal handy for such moments. Jot down your thoughts after an event to combine later with photos you've taken, sketch out a concept you had in a dream, or pin in a swatch of beautiful fabric. Don't get hung up on your journal being perfect—just keep it a fast and friendly tool for your eyes only! Then, when planning your layouts, you can flip through your notes to rev up your creativity.

Buy or create an inspiration journal that is worthy of your creative ideas and that you will enjoy using. I use a pretty, cloth-covered three-ring binder from my little company, Green Pear Studio. Inside, clippings, sketches, swatches and other embellishments are adhered to construction paper and then placed into page protectors. Tabbed dividers keep the ideas organized into sections for easy access later. My sections include typography, color schemes, textures, journaling, motifs and compositions.

sources for inspiration

* magazine ads and articles, both general and scrapbook related—for page designs, text arrangements or color combinations

* favorite quotes, poems, Scriptures, song lyrics and titles

* flashes of recalled memories, smells and sounds

* things your children, friends and family members say

* paintings, sculpture and architecture

* shapes, colors and patterns on everyday objects

* natural beauty such as landscapes, sunrises and sunsets

* pleasing textures, color combinations or designs in textiles or clothing

* accumulated lists, such as "Things I Love About My Husband"

* eye-catching greeting cards, wrapping paper, brochures, etc.

1 introduction to design

PHOTOS

5 reasons Sarah loves dandelions:

1. In springtime, you can find lots of them to pick
2. They look cute tucked behind your ear
3. Dandelion bouquets make nice presents for people you love
4. You can use them as makeup (for a sunny glow)
5. Dandelions are so bright and cheery!

Dandelion days

May 2005
Billings,
Montana

On this page showcasing a favorite springtime pursuit of my niece, the elements and principles of design were used to create a successful layout. It contains a balanced composition with a clear focal point, with a color scheme and accents that complement each other and the theme. The title and personal journaling draw in the viewer and contribute to the story of the page.

Supplies: Pink, yellow cardstocks · Patterned papers: brown, yellow designs (KI Memories), cloud (Frances Meyer), pink floral (Keeping Memories Alive), greet dot · Ribbon (Doodlebug Design) · Buttons · Thread · Foam adhesive · Impervious font

"Knowledge of the laws of design need not imprison, it can liberate from indecision."
—Johannes Itten

introduction

Build artistic expressions on a foundation of design theory

I'll let you in on a secret. The key to becoming a better scrapbook artist does not lie in owning the latest products, having a fancy workspace or even having lots of time to scrapbook. The key is becoming a better designer.

Chances are you like some layouts in your albums better than others. And when you read scrapbook magazines or look through your friends' albums, there's no doubt that certain pages stand out as especially well done. While personal taste plays a part in what draws you to certain pages, there is an underlying factor that all successful layouts have in common. What do you suppose that common denominator is? You guessed it: good design.

Good design begins with an understanding of design theory. Design theory is a set of established concepts as they apply to creating a composition. The building blocks of a composition are the elements of design: line, shape, space, texture and color. These elements are assembled into layouts using the principles of design: emphasis and focal point, proportion and scale, rhythm, balance and unity. An art student in any part of the world will likely embark on courses based on these universal concepts. Whether you are a painter, a graphic designer, a sculptor, a photographer, an architect, or, yes, a scrapbooker, your work will benefit from studying the philosophy of design.

Studying design theory will teach you why certain designs work, as well as why others are not successful. You'll be able to critique your own work and that of others, which will in turn allow you to develop your design skills.

Don't be afraid that employing design theory will be cumbersome or difficult or will reign in your creative freedom. Rather, its purpose is to give you tried-and-true tools that can be used to produce your most satisfying and spectacular artistic expressions. By building layouts with design guidelines, you will have a solid foundation upon which you can experiment, grow as an artist and even break the rules.

By breaking down design theory into specific topics and relating them directly to scrapbooking, you will quickly become educated in layout design. While some aspects of artistic talent are innate, I believe that good design can be learned with practice. Use this book to do just that—learn the elements and principles of design as they relate to the art of scrapbooking. Are you ready to become a better designer? Then let's get started!

study great pages

Examine layouts that catch your eye. Ask yourself what makes these pages successful. Chances are you'll notice the same elements that *Memory Makers* editors do when they review layouts for publication. As a former editor, here's what compelled me to either pick or pass on a page.

pick:

· Originality in layout concept

· Quality craftsmanship: sturdy construction, attention to detail

· First look piques interest in the story

· Clear, eye-catching photos

· Compelling title and journaling

· Well-planned and executed composition

· Well-chosen colors and accents that carry out the theme

pass:

· An unbalanced and/or disproportionate composition

· Floating elements

· Poor craftsmanship: crooked cuts, exposed adhesive, messy writing

· Forced design style for the sake of trendiness

· Lack of journaling and/or title

· Lack of unity, including conflicting elements and moods

· Lack of focal point

the elements of design

A designer's building blocks

✳ **line:** a series of points or a moving dot; a form that has length and very limited width

✳ **shape:** a visually perceived element created by either an edge, an enclosed line or by an area of color

✳ **space:** the area in which a design is created and interacts

✳ **texture:** the surface quality of an object

✳ **color:** the aspect of an object that is created by differing qualities of light reflected or emitted by the object

the principles of design

Tools that build the elements into a composition

✳ **emphasis and focal point:** an area of interest, attention and focus

✳ **proportion and scale:** the relationship of objects according to their size

✳ **rhythm:** the regular repetition of elements to produce the look and feel of movement and help unify a design

✳ **balance:** the equal distribution of visual weight

✳ **unity:** the arrangement of the parts of a design into a whole; the quality of being in accord

elements of a layout design

Is there a formula for a successful layout? These three illustrations demonstrate how the presence, or absence, of certain design elements separates a so-so layout from a great one.

not successful: While the photos are cute and the individual pieces of this layout are attractive and trendy, the combined result is nothing special.

✺ Unbalanced, bland composition with no focal point

✺ Pattern distracts from photos rather than complements

✺ Weak, disproportionate title

✺ Lack of journaling does not support photos' story

✺ Floating elements that lack unity

Supplies: Pink cardstock · Floral paper (Colors by Design) · Epoxy letters (Me & My Big Ideas) · Silk flowers (Doodlebug Design) · Ribbon · Buttons · Ivory thread

just average: The choice of elements and overall composition have improved, but they still do not create a dynamic design.

✺ Title is stronger but lacks interest

✺ No clear focal point

✺ Little contrast in color values makes page feel busy

✺ Impersonal journaling has little impact

✺ Color and composition choices are better, but predictable and lacking spark

Supplies: Pink, white cardstocks · Pink polka dot paper (Making Memories) · Floral, yellow dot paper (Bo-Bunny) · Flowers (Prima) · Buttons · Thread · Dateline font

successful: These design choices allow the photos to take center stage in an eye-catching composition.

✺ Playful, personal, accessible journaling

✺ Balanced composition with a clear focal point

✺ Colors complement the photos and carry out the theme

✺ Page embellishments accent photos and add to mood

✺ Eye-catching page title

Supplies: Pink, yellow cardstocks · Patterned papers: brown and yellow designs (KI Memories), cloud (Frances Meyer), pink floral (Keeping Memories Alive), green dot · Ribbon (Doodlebug Design) · Buttons · Thread · Foam adhesive · Impervious font

Recipe for Country Boy Stew

Ingredients:
1 energetic boy (age 9)
1 big black dog (Labrador Retriever recommended)
1 bicycle
1 cottage in rural village, situated on large property consisting of many derelict outbuildings, a pond, a stream, a graveyard, several fields and abundant varieties of vegetation and large trees
1 generous pinch imagination

Instructions:
Mix all ingredients thoroughly. Allow several hours of outdoor adventures, including tree climbing, hunting & fishing expeditions and exploring secret hideaways, until boy and dog return home hungry, grubby and tired. Top off with hearty food, a hot bath, a thrilling bedtime story and a good night's sleep. Repeat daily.

Oscar & Bruce
September 2005

a Boy's Life

Somerset Style

The steps of the design process can add up to a well-planned, successful layout. The six simple steps address picking photographs, writing journaling, choosing supplies, sketching a composition, testing out the design, and analyzing the end result. Creating your own effective design process allows you to make smart design choices.

the design process

An effective step-by-step plan adds up to successful design decisions

While in art school, I was taught design method and self-evaluation in a rigorous manner. My professors' goal was to make design analysis second nature. It worked! I definitely follow a certain process when I am creating, but I rarely notice it anymore because it has become intuitive. Through studying design in a deliberate, systematic way, the process becomes intrinsic.

Whether trained artists or passionate novices, all scrapbookers employ their own kinds of design processes while creating pages. They just may not be aware of them and therefore are not able to explain what their steps are. You, too, have a design process, even if you don't realize it! Each choice you make along the way contributes to your finished design. By studying the process, you can gain a better understanding of how you make design decisions. Before you begin learning about the elements and principles of design, it is helpful to first consider your own creative workflow.

To discover your personal design process, take conscious note of it the next couple of times you work on a project. Is your design process helping you complete pages, or is it getting in the way? What are you learning about your design skills, personal style, and strengths and weaknesses? By taking the time to analyze step-by-step how you create, you can determine if you are working in the most effective manner and where you would like to strengthen your skills. If you find that you are skipping a step or that it may work better for you to do certain steps in a different order, make a plan to rework your creation process when you do your next layout. Implement the new agenda and see how it goes; then revise again if needed. In short order, you will be working more efficiently and making better design decisions. It won't take long before your new process becomes second nature to you.

I utilize each step of the design process in this chapter to analyze how the different parts of a page will synchronize with one another. I judge a layout based on whether it "sings" to me when it is complete. Does the sum of its parts come together harmoniously in the design? In this section, I will take you through the steps of my own design process (based on a traditional model) while creating a layout. Although this model is not the only right way to approach a design, use it as a template that can be adapted to suit your personal creative style.

design process steps

Refer to this process as you create to help make well-designed scrapbook pages every time.

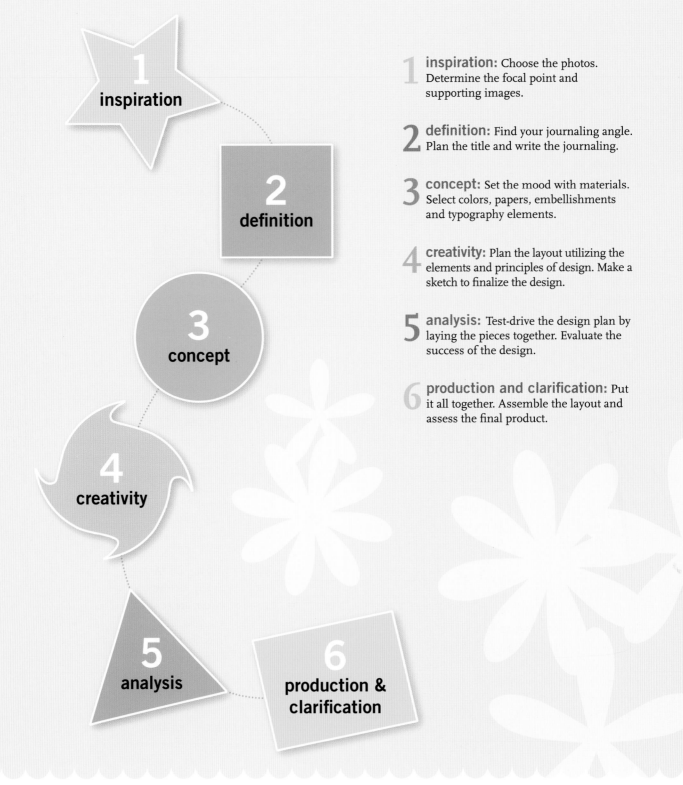

1 inspiration: Choose the photos. Determine the focal point and supporting images.

2 definition: Find your journaling angle. Plan the title and write the journaling.

3 concept: Set the mood with materials. Select colors, papers, embellishments and typography elements.

4 creativity: Plan the layout utilizing the elements and principles of design. Make a sketch to finalize the design.

5 analysis: Test-drive the design plan by laying the pieces together. Evaluate the success of the design.

6 production and clarification: Put it all together. Assemble the layout and assess the final product.

Photos inspire most of the elements of a layout, so begin your design process by reviewing pictures. If you could use only one photo, which would it be? Choose that photograph as your focal point, with other shots acting as supporting players.

1
inspiration

choose the images

Since the core of most layouts is their photographs, inspiration begins by reviewing your pictures. You don't need to scrapbook every photo. Just choose the photos that best get your message across and draw in the viewer. Selected images should be clear, good quality, well composed and engaging. Think of yourself as a photojournalist; you have limited space to tell a story in a dynamic way. What are your best choices to meet that goal? If you could use only one photo, which would it be? This is your focal-point photograph, and will be the axis of the design. Then critically consider secondary images that will support your story.

Once your photos are chosen, consider how they could benefit from cropping or resizing in order to keep the focus on the main subject or enhance the theme of the layout. You can implement these modifications later in the design process when their final dimensions have been determined.

When I began working on "A Boy's Life" (page 20), I first looked through my pictures. These photos of my husband's nephew, Oscar, are some of my favorites from our trip to England last year. I had taken several shots of Oscar and his dog Bruce, but I especially loved those that showed the affable interaction between them, so the top left photo (above) was a clear choice for the focal point. The photo of Oscar on a bicycle made a good supporting image. I knew I wanted the focal point photo to be cropped in close and printed large, but for this stage, I estimated the size for it and the supporting photo.

Once you have chosen the photos for your layout, think about what story they tell. Jot down notes and key words that will then guide you in writing your journaling. Check your final journaling for grammar and spelling.

vacation memories or make you realize how grown-up your toddler has become? Journaling adds another layer of meaning by allowing people to "see" your thoughts with words.

The words chosen for the layout's title are also very important. The title should capture the essence of your photos, give an overview of the layout and draw interest. If you're having trouble writing a title, review title idea books, scrapbook Web sites, song lyrics and movie titles for inspiration. A good title can be anything from a clever pun to a straightforward descriptor.

Working on the title and journaling early in the design process will ensure that they are in sync with the rest of the layout. Advance planning with photos and journaling helps define the message you want to convey and sets the tone for upcoming design decisions. You will also know in advance approximately how much space to plan for the typography elements.

While I could have simply described the circumstances surrounding my photos of Oscar, I realized that the real story is how happy he is living in the country and what he likes to do there. This concept makes the best journaling angle. I jotted down some notes taken from observations of and conversations with Oscar, his parents and his grandmother. Although I started by writing a traditional paragraph, I was inspired to compose it in the form of a recipe. This is often how the writing process goes—once you start writing, a more original or defined concept will enter your mind. Go with it! I then wrote recipe-style journaling on the computer and edited the text for spelling and grammar. I chose a title that was inspired by a movie and would work well with the layout's story and recipe concept.

2
definition

find your journaling angle

Journaling can sometimes feel time-consuming and difficult, but no layout is complete without it. To define the layout's message, look at the photos you have just chosen. What story do they tell? Is this an event-centered page, a character study, or the expression of an emotion? If you were telling a friend about these photos, what would you say? This kind of information is the story behind the photos and should be reflected in your journaling.

At a minimum, your journaling should answer who, what, where, when, why and how. Even better, the journaling should include personal insights and details one can visualize. You may have heard the adage "Show, don't tell," in English class. This rule for good writing also holds true with your scrapbook journaling. Don't just say, "The ocean was beautiful." Describe your senses and emotions to *show* what made it beautiful to you. Did you love the way the sun reflected off the water, or relish the sound of the waves crashing to shore? Did it bring back childhood

Let your photos and journaling inspire your choice of papers, embellishments and typography style that will best set the mood and support the theme of your layout.

3 concept

set the mood

Now that you have established a message by choosing your photos and planning text, setting the tone of your layout should follow naturally. Think through the colors and themes that will express the mood you want to convey. Look at the photos and determine what colors will best suit them. Experiment with cardstock colors by placing them behind your photos. Decide what color will work best as your background, photo mats and accent colors. Determine if patterned paper will add to the mood. If so, look for patterns that coordinate with solid colors as well as the photos. Now think about what embellishments, lettering styles and textures will add to the mood you are setting. The colors and materials you choose should work in harmony to set a mood that's appropriate to your message.

I wanted to echo the vibrant colors and organic materials that are the backdrops of both my photos and this aspect of Oscar's life. In addition, I wanted the materials to have a masculine feel. I looked through my paper stash and picked out two lively, masculine patterns in a blue, green and yellow color scheme that complemented the photos. I chose accents that had subtle homespun textures but were not overtly rustic, such as twill, torn fabric ribbon, twine and wooden buttons. I decided it was appropriate to incorporate the recipe journaling onto schoolboy-like notebook paper rather than a cooking-recipe-card format. With the notebook paper and masculine mood in mind, I chose a handwriting-style font for the journaling and a coordinating title font.

photo
Oscar on
bike

photo
Oscar & Bruce

Oscar & Bruce

a Boys Life

Somerset
Style

Sketch a small-scale version of your potential page design and evaluate how the basic elements interact. By looking at the sketch, you can identify—and fix—many design flaws before you ever get out the scissors.

4

creativity

plan the layout

With papers and embellishments chosen, it's time to pull them together with your photos and start planning a preliminary design. While narrowing down your composition, consider the elements and principles of design. The viewer's eye should flow naturally through the layout from the focal point to the supporting elements. By making a plan at this stage, you can easily identify and correct many design problems long before photos are cropped and adhered to the page.

Creating a sketch of your plan is helpful during this process. You can draw a sketch by hand or design it on the computer. A sketch is also useful to determine sizes for photographs and other parts of the design. While the initial sketch may change as the design evolves, it allows you to conceptualize how elements such as line and shape will interact within the layout's space. You may even want to challenge yourself to do more than one sketch so you can compare multiple approaches.

I made some preliminary sketches for "A Boy's Life" that resulted in the idea to place the supporting photo on a tag suspended from a twig. I then worked on a final sketch, placing the large focal photo on the right because I wanted Oscar to be facing into the page. The tag at the upper left was anchored from a twig and a horizontal twill strip. The area below the tag was reserved for journaling, and the title was placed under the main photo. It is a simple composition, but the pieces fit together and ground each other well. The large photo next to smaller elements successfully balances the two sides of the design.

Before you adhere your page elements, do a test run and assemble them according to the final sketch. Now, evaluate the design. Does the page sing? If something isn't working, tweak the page and reevaluate the composition until you are happy with the results.

Recipe for Country Boy Stew

Ingredients:
1 energetic boy (age 9)
1 big black dog (Labrador Retriever recommended)
1 bicycle
1 cottage in rural village, situated on large property consisting of many derelict outbuildings, a pond, a stream, a graveyard, several fields and abundant varieties of vegetation and large trees
1 generous pinch imagination

Instructions:
Mix all ingredients thoroughly. Allow several hours of outdoor adventures, including tree climbing, hunting & fishing expeditions and exploring secret hideaways, until boy and dog return home hungry, grubby and tired. Top off with hearty food, a hot bath, a thrilling bedtime story and a good night's sleep. Repeat daily.

5 analysis

evaluate the parts

You've done your pre-planning, so now it's time for a practice run. With adhesive still on hold, go ahead and arrange the pieces of the layout according to your sketch. First, arrange any background pieces and mat the photos. Make (or mock up) any embellishments, such as a stamped image or title letters. Lay the accents on the page and play around with them until you are satisfied with their placement.

Next, fine-tune the journaling space. Although you have planned it in your sketch and know its approximate size, this stage is the best time to finalize it. Measure the space and use those measurements to create the journaling block on the computer or by hand. Even if you plan to handwrite the journaling, make a rough draft first to allow for editing. Do a test by printing or writing the journaling as it will appear on the layout and making sure it fits

properly. When you are satisfied, make a final version.

After you have all the parts arranged, analyze the layout. Ask yourself the self-evaluation questions and perform the squint test explained on page 29. Is the layout singing? If not, what is the problem? Keep tweaking the design and reevaluating the outcome until you are satisfied with the results.

Using my layout sketch as a guide, I first printed out the two photos and cut the papers to the correct size. Next, I laid all the pieces down according to the design, without any adhesive. I was then able to cut the twig and twill to the correct lengths. When I was happy with the overall arrangement, I measured the journaling space and formatted my text accordingly on the computer. When testing the size of the journaling, I realized that the small photo needed to be moved up about ½" (1cm). It was an easy adjustment to make, and after doing so, I was satisfied with the revised arrangement.

For the final step of the design process, get out the adhesive and assemble the page. Do a final review and check your craftsmanship. Each step of the design process now pays off when the result is the successful execution of a family keepsake.

Supplies: Moss green, pale yellow, ivory cardstocks · Patterned papers (Basic Grey) · Moss green twill (Creek Bank Creations) · Gingham fabric · Twine · Wooden buttons (JHB International) · Twig (cleaned, dried in low oven and sprayed with varnish) · Green, gold, caramel dye ink (Stampin' Up!) · Foam adhesive · Kantor font · Lights Out BRK font

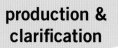

production & clarification

put it all together

Finally, it is time to get out your adhesive! Put all the elements in their places according to your design plan. At this point, everything should fit together smoothly with no surprises. When you are finished, take a step back and look at the layout. There should be very few problems since you have made thoughtful decisions in each step of the design process.

When assembling the final layout, I worked in layers from bottom to top, starting with the background papers and photo mats. I inked the paper edges with green for dimension, and put them in place along with the twill. I printed a final version of the journaling onto white cardstock, created the torn edge and stippled on brown ink to distress and soften its appearance. Next, I cut out the title font from patterned paper, matted each letter in green cardstock and adhered the pieces to the layout with foam adhesive. Last, the finishing touches of twine with wooden buttons, twig, fabric ribbon and small tags were added.

Once the layout is put together, check your craftsmanship. Nothing should distract from the overall design. Avoid stray pencil marks, messy penmanship, ragged cuts or excessive adhesive.

Take a few moments of self-evaluation and do a final squint test. Your design should now be singing a lovely tune, and you can admire the memory you've created using this step-by-step design process.

craftsmanship checklist

Don't forget that neatness counts! Go through this checklist for each layout.

- ❑ Pencil and other stray marks are erased
- ❑ All elements are evenly cut and aligned
- ❑ Journaling and title are neatly executed, legible and aligned
- ❑ No adhesive shows around the edges of the elements
- ❑ Cuts are clean and smooth
- ❑ Stamped images are crisp and well-defined
- ❑ Interactive elements fit together smoothly
- ❑ Layout is sturdy and well-adhered

the squint test

When you do the squint test, you are employing a scientific theory called the Gestalt Principle (isn't that cool?!). It states that our eyes see an object as a whole before we look at its individual parts. Stand back from your layout and squint your eyes. One scrapbooking friend suggests placing the layout on the floor and squinting down at it while standing on a chair for a proper viewing distance. Analyze the impressions you get from the blurred form, and ask yourself the following questions:

✻ 1 **Is my focal point easy to identify?**

✻ 2 **Is the layout visually balanced from side to side and top to bottom?**

✻ 3 **Are there any jarring spots or awkward empty spaces?**

self-evaluation guide

* Does my title attract the viewer and elicit interest?

* Is my journaling legible and tidy, and does it express my theme?

* Have I completed the craftsmanship checklist (on page 28)?

* Are my photographs aesthetically sound, relevant to my story and of good quality?

* Do the colors complement the photos and fit with the mood of the layout?

* Do my embellishments add to or detract from the theme of the page? Do they overwhelm or emphasize the photos?

* Are there floating elements that need to be anchored?

* Does the eye move through the design, or is the layout static or confusing?

* Do all parts of the layout flow together as a whole?

* Does the layout tell the story I would want to convey if I was not present?

elements of

design

2

While Mum and Dad were visiting for the weekend, we took a trip downtown one evening. We stopped by the Denver Art Museum to check out the architecture of their new addition. This orange erector set-like sculpture lives in the courtyard between the museum and the Central Library. Suddenly Dad started scaling the sculpture and perched on one of the crosspieces. His spontaneous climb and the resulting photos remind me of one of Dad's mottos: Keep pressing in and living upward. March 2006

Living Upward

This sketch shows the line and shape that make up this layout's underlying design. The dynamic shapes shown in the photograph are extended into the design space to create an eye-catching effect. Additionally, dynamic negative spaces are created in the white areas in between the orange shapes. The font design and text format were chosen to echo the line qualities present elsewhere in the composition.

Supplies: White, dark orange cardstock · Black pen · Colored pencils · Chrome Yellow font

line, shape & space

Structure a layout with these core design elements

My father was an architect when I was a child. In addition to an office in town, he had one in our loft at home. I would often head up the spiral staircase to his perch to watch him at his drafting table (those were the days before computer-aided design programs). The slide-rule suspended across the table on wires made a whooshing noise as it went up and down to mark horizontal lines. He used many intriguing tools: special rulers to make verticals, diagonals and circles, textural rubber stamps to indicate trees, and even templates to represent tiny appliances. His office smelled like blueprint toner, pencil lead and paper. I loved the sounds, tools and smells in Dad's space, but most of all I loved to see his marks grow into a design. It was magical how a series of lines, shapes and spaces would come together to create a building.

An architectural drawing represents the underlying structure of a house through its arrangement of the most basic elements of design: line, shape and space. Scrapbook pages are built using the same elements. All other aspects of a layout are built upon the foundation you create with line, shape and space.

Line is the basic building block of any design. A line consists of a series of points, or as twentieth-century artist Paul Klee aptly described it: "A line is a dot that went for a walk." It has definite length and limited width.

While a series of dots form a line, lines converge to create shapes. A shape is a visually perceived element created by either an edge, an enclosed line or by an area of color. It is the arrangement of these shapes that forms a composition.

Whether curvy or straight, round or square, lines and shapes have their own personalities that impact the mood of a design. They are able to show movement, provide structure and suggest recognizable forms.

Space is the area in which a design is created and interacts. Lines and shapes exist within a specific space. They define the space they inhabit through their character and placement. The space around and between lines and shapes becomes its own element within a composition.

When a scrapbook layout is represented as a simple sketch, its basic structure can easily be seen. The page's design is boiled down to an arrangement of lines and shapes within the composition space. The sketched version of "Living Upward" on page 32 shows the basic line and shape of the layout. Line, shape and space are the most fundamental elements of design. Together, they create the basic blueprint of a layout and suggest its underlying character.

line, space and shape in layouts

On scrapbook layouts, line and shape are created mainly by the edges of the elements on the page. These edges are present where two papers or colors meet, in the contour of the page embellishments and anywhere there is a change in color value.

In addition, line and shape exist within the materials on the page in the form of patterned paper designs, embellishment characteristics and text treatments. Patterns and embellishments are made up of lines and shapes, and letters of the alphabet are linear expressions.

In scrapbook design, space exists within the surface area of the layout itself. That space has limited depth, depending on the thickness of the layout. Its surface area is defined by the page's dimensions and whether the layout is a single or a double spread.

types of lines

There are three basic types of line: actual, implied and psychic. An actual line is deliberate and obvious to the eye. Look at the tags below. On the left tag, actual lines exist in the form of repeated paper strips. Hand-drawn doodles and a striped background are also examples of actual lines.

An implied line is created when the eye automatically connects a series of points. A dotted line is a simple example. Implied lines can also create implied shapes within a design. On the middle tag, an implied visual triangle is created between the points made by the three coffee cups.

line types

actual lines   **implied lines**   **psychic lines**

Supplies: Brown, ivory cardstocks · Green check paper · All other patterned papers (K & Company) · Stamps: spoon (Wordsworth), coffee beans, small coffee cup (Rubber Stamps of America), large coffee cup (Rubberstamp Ave.) · ColorBox Fluid Chalk Chestnut Roan ink (Clearsnap) · Colored pencils · Brown thread · Lace · Foam adhesive

A psychic line is a mental connection between two elements that creates a visual line where there is no actual or implied line present. On the right tag, a psychic line exists between the spoon and the coffee beans. The edge of the spoon lip directs your eye to the coffee beans, creating a psychic line.

No matter what type of line a design employs, lines move the eye around the composition. This movement can be controlled by the designer. As you design a layout, anticipate where lines will exist and intersect and the kind of visual movement they will create.

line quality

Line qualities express mood and movement. Decide on a mood that fits the theme of your layout. Then choose line qualities to express that feeling.

Regardless of which type of line you are using, lines fall into two quality categories: rectilinear and curvi-linear. A rectilinear line is regular, precise and geometric. For example, straight and zigzag lines are rectilinear. Curvilinear lines are curving and twisting, reflecting the organic shapes of nature, such as spirals and waves.

Whether rectilinear or curvilinear, line character is further determined by its direction, texture and spacing. In a design, the directions of lines have associated visual characteristics. See each direction in the set of tags on page 37. Horizontal lines imply calmness and stability. Vertical lines suggest aspiration and activity. Diagonal lines convey dynamic movement and energy. Repeated vertical lines in the layout "Expressive Nature" on page 38 create a mood of subtle liveliness.

Line textures can create edge effects that contribute to a mood. Compare the hard, shiny edge of a strip of metal to the soft, wispy torn edge of mulberry paper. Techniques such as inking, tearing and crumpling can each produce a distinctive edge effect.

rectilinear lines

curvilinear lines

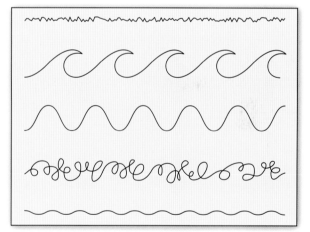

geometric shapes

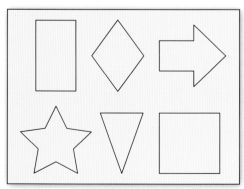

Each type of line and shape has its own character, as represented in this chart. Contrast the angular, precise quality of the rectilinear lines and geometric shapes to the natural, loose look of the curvilinear lines and organic shapes.

natural/organic shapes

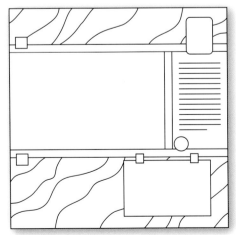

A hard-edged, graphic feel is created in this layout with precise line contours and high-contrast edges, which play against the curvilinear nature of the zebra stripes. The white areas between the stripes create distinctive patterns of negative space. The diagonal direction of the stripes echoes the wild attitude of the animals in the photo.

PHOTO AND JOURNALING: DANIELLE ANDRUS

Supplies: Black, white, purple cardstocks · Tilez acrylic tag (Junkitz) · Zebra stamp (Rubberstamp Ave.) · StazOn black solvent ink (Tsukineko) · Ribbon · Hinges · Brads · Flair zebra accent (Magic Scraps) · Backhand Brush font

line direction

Line direction can influence the energy level found in a design. Although the materials of these three tags are similar, the line direction of each piece conveys a different statement. Horizontal lines suggest calmness and stability. Vertical lines project aspiration and activity. Diagonal lines express dynamic movement and energy.

| **horizontal** | **vertical** | **diagonal** |

Supplies: Brown, ivory cardstocks · Green check paper · All other patterned papers (K & Company) · Stamps: triangular coffee label (Stampa Rosa), java paper cup (Rubber Stamps of America), "Let's have Coffee" (Wordsworth), small coffee cup (100 Proof Press) · ColorBox Fluid Chalk Chestnut Roan ink (Clearsnap) · Colored pencils · Buttons · Brown thread · Lace · Foam adhesive

shape quality

Since shapes are made of lines, their basic categories are similar. But instead of being described as rectilinear or curvilinear, shapes are either geometric or organic. Geometric shapes are characterized by angular corners and contained contours. While geometric shapes can be found in nature, these shapes often have a man-made, synthetic feel to them. An organic shape is derived from a form that is natural in appearance, such as a shell or leaf.

When choosing shapes for a design, consider the mood you would like to convey. Think of adjectives for that mood and then picture shapes that evoke corresponding feelings. You can also look to your photos for inspiration. There may be interesting shapes in the photos that could be echoed in the design.

aspects of space

Space can be used effectively as a graphic element in a design. Because space is created around and through lines and shapes, its power lies within the way those components work together, creating spatial relationships. With space, what is absent can be just as important as what is present.

Notice that the intentional, or positive, shapes in a design have spaces between and around them. These areas are called negative spaces, which in turn create their own interesting shapes in a design. On "Saucy Stripes" on the opposite page, the negative white spaces create shapes as distinctive as the positive black stripes. Maintain an awareness, and thus control, of how negative space is working within your design.

expressive nature

happy

sassy

silly

Whatever Zoe is thinking shows on her face, constantly full of one emotion or another. Always animated, Zoe's face can change in a heartbeat to reflect her thoughts and moods—from wild to sweet, excited to curious, happy to mad, bubbly to shy. She has crinkled her nose for dramatic effect since she was a baby and has particular faces just for the camera. With her big blue eyes and ready expressions, Zoe clearly communicates her feelings whether or not she says a word.

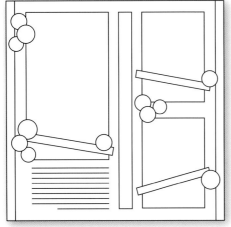

Line and shape characteristics can support the mood of a design. The repeated vertical lines on this layout convey an active feeling. The line and shape quality throughout the design is soft and natural to reflect the organic, feminine mood, as seen in the torn paper edges, frayed fabric and script font.

PHOTOS: MICHELLE PENDLETON

Supplies: Red cardstock · Patterned papers: floral (Keeping Memories Alive), red quilt (Memories Complete) · Red mulberry paper · Fabric sheet (FiberMark) · Rust twill (Creek Bank Creations) · Rub-on letters (Making Memories) · Transparency (Grafix) · Rust thread · Chalk · Foam adhesive · Computer fonts

Open space (also called white space) is an area intentionally left empty in a composition. This device provides a place for the eye to rest and can also result in dramatic effects. In addition, open spaces can contribute to a design's balance and lend punch to a focal point. For example, "Living Upward" (page 32), uses open space as an important part of its composition.

vary line & shape for interest

When using line and shape, follow this basic design rule: If a series of identical lines or shapes is repeated, always include one element that is different among them. Doing so will add variety to your layout and thus create successful results. When working with rectilinear and curvilinear lines, choose one line type to be dominant in the design. Let the other line type act as visual contrast in small doses or to emphasize the focal point.

With shapes, you can vary their conventional qualities for unexpected combinations. Natural shapes need not always have soft edges. Geometric shapes could be created in fluffy textures. You might choose to use predominately organic shapes but then execute them in crisp, defined lines. This is the case in "Saucy Stripes" (page 36). While the zebra stripes themselves are curvilinear in nature, the look here is anything but soft. The stark contrast of the color scheme and the precise contours of the striped background create an overall dramatic, graphic look.

By making mental or actual sketches of your layouts, you can see how the line, shape and space of their structure interact. This will allow you to break down your page's composition, ensuring well-designed pages every time.

implement innovative structure

Looking for some shapely inspiration?
Try one of these approaches when planning line, shape and space in a composition:

＊ go above and beyond
With a photo that crops through an interesting shape or pattern, you could continue that shape beyond the picture plane and into the composition space for a striking effect. (See "Living Upward," page 32.)

＊ think outside the box
Would your photos benefit from being a shape other than rectangular or square? Circles and ovals can be especially versatile, and used in a modern, well-designed way, other shapes might create a fresh and stunning effect. Dust off your old shape-making tools to experiment with new approaches.

＊ craft form-fitting text
Compose a layout's title and journaling to reflect shapes in the design. Look beyond the typical methods of formatting text, such as a journaling block or vertical title. Think about unconventional ways to incorporate text into the other shapes on the page. Choose lettering styles that share the same line qualities.

＊ do a real-estate adjustment
If you tend to fill every inch of a layout, challenge yourself to create a layout that utilizes open space as a prominent design feature. This extreme departure from your usual approach will give you a new perspective.

＊ find a fresh angle
Trim one side of the focal point photo in a different angle or shape to create a dramatic effect. For instance, cut one side into a convex curve or slice off a piece at a deep slant.

pleased to *meet* you

Tom met his younger nephew Alexander for the first time when we visited England in early fall of 2005. The little boy was shy around us at first, but it didn't take long before Alexander returned to his usual two-year self, full of curiosity and energy. Watching him play outside with joyous abandon and wide-eyed innocence, Tom observed that it is as if there is still a bit of heaven about him that he has not grown away from yet. Tom dubbed him the "mischievous cherub", and commented that Alexander favors Uncle John in appearance. He seems to be as charming as Uncle John as well!

Natural textures pop against saturated colors on this page about my husband and his nephew. Combine unrefined, robust elements from the natural world, such as wood, jute and dried botanicals, to complement down-to-earth subjects, such as outdoor activities, seasons and the zoo.

Supplies: Turquoise cardstock · Patterned papers (K & Company) · Woven grass paper (Be Unique) · Transparency (Grafix) · Skeleton leaves · Wooden buttons (JHB International) · Yellow mulberry mesh (ScrapArts) · Pressed flowers (Nature's Pressed) · Bamboo clips (Anima Designs) · Jute rickrack · Wooden beads · Turquoise glass beads (Blue Moon Beads) · Thread · Twine · Photo corners · Acrylic paint · Foam adhesive (3L) · BlackJack font · Oktoberfest font

texture

Add dimension and support theme with tactile elements

ranging from the tender softness of baby skin to the scratchy grit of sandpaper, the dense richness of a pet's fur to the rigid slickness of a computer keyboard, our sense of touch continuously chronicles a variety of textures. Even when we don't actually touch an object, our eyes register its textural appearance based on memories of tactile experiences. By both real and visual touch, we encounter an endless number of objects every day and record their surface qualities. Touch elicits an array of emotional reactions to different kinds of textures. Scrapbook artists can tap into that power of texture when creating their layouts.

Simply defined, texture is the surface quality of an object. Although texture is an element of design along with color, line, shape and space, it is unique because it involves touch as well as sight. It can evoke both a sensory reaction and an emotional response. Think of the way you feel about certain textures. Do slimy or prickly textures repel while fluffy or silky ones attract? Can different versions of smooth surfaces seem either sterile (stainless steel) or sophisticated (marble), while rough ones can feel either natural (wood grain) or primitive (grass matting)? Why does bunny fur elicit petting while a snake's skin usually incites repulsion? Whatever your response to certain textures, the texture of an object creates a reaction.

tactile versus implied texture

Let's look at the two kinds of textures that exist in design: tactile and implied. Tactile textures can be felt as well as seen. These are touchable surfaces such as ribbed corduroy fabric or pebbled handmade paper. When looking at a tactile texture, light brings out its character. The higher the relief of a texture, the more visual contrast will be created as light hits it, just like a deeper texture is easier to feel.

Implied textures have a textural appearance that is suggested to the eye but cannot actually be felt. The illusion of texture is produced by a pattern, which the eye interprets as some type of surface. The pattern may simply create an abstract textural effect, like stripes, or represent a real texture, like crackled paint. Either way, value contrasts in the pattern give the illusion of dimension. Examples of implied texture are patterned paper that looks like corrugated cardboard, a transparency overlay with the line quality of chicken wire or a sticker with a crosshatch surface reminiscent of fabric weave.

contribute to theme & mood

Due to the emotive component of texture, it can be an effective tool to support a layout's theme and create a mood. Think about the story of your photos and journaling and then consider what kind of textures will complement that statement. Next, choose corresponding materials for the page.

The five layouts in this chapter each use a different set of textures. Next to each layout is a grouping that represents the kind of textures it employs. Each grouping creates a unique textural environment that supports the mood of the page. If you looked at the grouping on its own, you could probably make a good guess at the mood its layout would have. If textures can tell you that much on their own, consider how effective they can be in a design when combined with your photos and words.

For "Boys Rock" on page 45, a hip, urban mood was created with industrial, man-made textures. Modern surfaces such as plastic, metal, wire and duct tape work together to create a contemporary environment appropriate for the subject matter. The result is a playful rock-and-roll look, with a funky ball chain border and wire and rivets combined to echo guitar frets. Compare how different this layout would feel if it had been created using the same set of textures as the "Little Six" layout on page 44. In contrast to the sleek, masculine textures of "Boys Rock," this layout employs soft, feminine textures to create an opposite mood. By correlating texture associations with the layout's theme, each layout uses textures that create an appropriate mood for its design.

texture in design

In addition to supporting a theme or mood, use texture to create dimension and visual interest in a design. The eye is drawn to the value contrast within a texture or pattern. Use

Asian textures echo the little girls' apparel on this layout. A sleek brocade fabric with an oriental floral motif contrasts against the nubby grass paper and bamboo pieces. Ornate Chinese coins, silky ribbon, a Mizuhiki paper cord flower and a lacquered title add finishing touches to the exotic texture environment. Pages about travel or cultural events would also benefit from ethnic textures.

PHOTOS: KEN TRUJILLO

Supplies: Dark pink cardstock (Prism Papers) · Satin brocade fabric · Bamboo paper (Be Unique) · Transparency (Grafix) · Chinese coins (Dove of the East) · Bamboo · Ribbon (May Arts) · Mizuhiki paper cord flower embellishment (Yasutomo) · Gold photo corners (Canson) · Clear gloss medium (Sakura Hobby Craft) · Pink thread · Super Tape, Heat N Bond Lite iron-on fabric adhesive (Therm O Web) · Black foam adhesive (EK Success) · Ondine font

contrasting textures to effectively highlight a focal point, generate variety, or build rhythm and movement into a composition. On the layout "China Dolls" on the opposite page, the sleek brocade fabric is played off the organic grass paper and bamboo pieces, creating visual interest through contrast. The striking combination emphasizes the exotic beauty of the textures on the page and in the photographs. "Dreams" (below) creates movement with rows of horizontal ribbons, while the repeated borders of beads, buttons or dried flowers create rhythm on "Pleased to Meet You" (page 40).

Regardless of your style or skill level, you can use texture to support a page theme or create visual interest. Whether it is as subtle as the linen-like cardstock or as dramatic as modeling paste, the inclusion of texture brings pleasing dimension and emotion to page designs. Explore the surface qualities all around you and use those textures to express the story of your scrapbook memories.

Jillian Jo

As you grow up
in fields of gold in Idaho
Visions of lights on
Broadway fill your hopes
My daughter, forever
beautiful and so determined
May your unwavering spirit take
you everywhere you can dream.

dreams

Mix the luxurious textures of velvet, brocade and tapestry with ornate metal accents for lavish backdrops with formal appeal, perfect for holiday, heritage and special event pages. Such textures also work well for dressed-up feminine layouts like this one, where they are combined with a rich color palette.

PHOTOS: APRIL ANDERTON

Supplies: Copper crinkle paper (Emagination Crafts) · Burgundy velvet paper (Hot Off The Press) · Transparency (Grafix) · Copper label holder, buckles, brads (Nunn Design) · Life's Journey copper photo corners, hinges (K & Company) · Ribbon (Offray) · Velvet leaf, mother of pearl buttons (Artchix Studio) · Shoe charms (Boxer Scrapbook Productions) · Magic Metallic copper paint (Mayco) · Seed beads · Thread · Foam adhesive · Dauphin font

Little

SIX MONTHS OLD ◦ JULY 1971

PRECIOUS

JOURNALING BY CONNIE

6 MEMORIES OF MY BABY KARI WITH THE BIG EYES, AT SIX MONTHS OLD:

1. **Naps & Cuddles:** You loved to rock and cuddle in the old orange and brown rocking chair. You took long naps. This was a huge blessing, since I was typing depositions at home for extra money and I would type like mad while you were asleep!
2. **On the Move:** You were crawling everywhere, including following big sister Lori around. Continually pulled yourself up using the fireplace hearth and trying to walk. I was afraid you were going to crack your head open on that rock ledge!
3. **Bedtime Wonder:** You started sleeping through the night at six weeks old (which was miraculous to us since Lori didn't sleep all night until she was two). You slept with a pink blankie with silky edging.
4. **Self Entertaining:** You were content to sit on the floor and play with toys for hours on your own. A favorite activity was pulling the Tupperware out of the bottom kitchen cupboard.
5. **Independent Nature:** In general, you were very independent. You wanted to feed yourself at this age. We couldn't keep you in your crib, as you would climb over the side.
6. **Easy Disposition:** You woke up with a smile and were a cheerful, happy baby. You never fussed unless you were hungry. We hardly knew you were around; you were such a good baby!

For this nostalgic baby girl page, textures with homespun appeal were chosen. Soft calico and gingham fabrics, ribbons and lace work together to create a look full of delicate charm. Journaling pulls out of a vellum envelope. Layer shabby chic textures such as polished cotton, pretty trims, silky petals, timeless pearls and filmy sheers to create a sweet, girlish mood.

JOURNALING: CONNIE HANSEN

Supplies: Pink, light brown cardstocks · Floral, gingham fabrics (Moda Fabrics) · Patterned papers: Liz King striped (EK Success), floral (Anna Griffin) · Vellum (Grafix) · Large silk flowers, photo corners (Heidi Swapp) · Small flower (Prima) · Stitched fabric accent (Autumn Leaves) · Woven tab (Scrapworks) · Ribbon (May Arts) · Trim · Lace · Pearl buttons · Thread · Heat N Bond Lite iron-on fabric adhesive (Therm O Web) · Foam adhesive (3L) · Lauren Script font · Organda MN font · Architect font

Objects with machine-made surfaces such as metal tags, wire and rivets, along with slick plastic labels and utilitarian duct tape, lend a contemporary feel to this design about a budding electric guitar player. Employ these types of textures for a variety of themes relating to urban life and modern technology.

PHOTOS AND JOURNALING: KELLI NOTO

Supplies: Black, teal cardstocks (WorldWin) · Vellum (Grafix) · Woven label (Me & My Big Ideas) · Guitar embellishment (Meri Meri) · Micro eyelets, silver eyelets, thick ball chain, metal rimmed tag, metal letter K (Making Memories) · Aluminum tag, keyhole, tickets (Anima Designs) · Bottle cap (Li'l Davis Designs) · Round silver tag, spiral clips, thin ball chain (Creative Impressions) · Metal mesh (Scrapyard 329) · White twill (Creek Bank Creations) · Label tape (Dymo) · Alphabet stamps (Picture Show) · Black dye ink · Silver wire · Jump rings · Duct tape · Foam adhesive · Another Typewriter font

design with texture

Try these ideas when adding textural elements to layouts:

❋ To take a design from flat to fabulous without a lot of fuss, incorporate low-dimension textures, such as fabric, handmade paper, mesh, ribbons and fiber.

❋ If a certain texture is impractical to use because it is too bulky or if there are archival concerns, consider using a pre-made faux textured product. Scanning objects to create you own *trompe-l'oeil* (fool the eye) effect will work also.

❋ Maximize visual impact with dramatic contrasts in surface qualities, such as soft against coarse or shiny against matte.

❋ Utilize hands-on techniques to create custom textures. Try techniques like inked or torn paper edges, collage, layering, rubber stamping, distressing and sewing. Adapt home decorating ideas such as crackle finish, glazes and sponging onto your pages with paint products made for paper.

❋ Check out sewing, hardware, art supply, clothing and stationery stores for unique texture ideas. Purchase items there for use on layouts or create a similar look with traditional scrapbooking supplies.

❋ Make sure the textures you include are appropriate for the page's theme. For example, modern Dymo label tape on "Dreams" (page 43), would have looked out of place, but it looks right at home with the industrial textures of "Boys Rock" (above).

Water Works

Steven & Sarah · July 02

What does the combination of sizzling hot summer days and two lively kids with a limited tolerance for indoor, air-conditioned activities add up to? The answer: wet and wild water fun! During the steamy temperatures of an above-average July, Steven and Sarah gave the garden hose a workout. Running through the sprinklers, having water fights or making sand pies on the patio--all were successfully employed to cool off and expend excess energy. Happy shrieks and squeals regularly emitted from the patio or yard, as the pair thoroughly soaked themselves once again

Grandma's House
Billings, Montana

On this playful page featuring my niece and nephew, the title is placed on a beribboned paper strip to provide definition against the background. A drop cap unifies the text and title and also provides a distinctive start to the journaling. Supporting date and location information is added on file folder-like tabs, while handwriting adds a personal touch to the computer fonts found elsewhere on the layout.

Supplies: Blue cardstocks (Prism Papers) · Patterned papers: teal sea horse (Paper Adventures), blue swirl (Creative Imaginations), Sarah Bond blue floral (Autumn Leaves) · Blue gingham fabric · Blue thread · Le Plume blue pen (Marvy) · Bordering Blue dye ink (Stampin' Up!) · Foam adhesive · Whackadoo font

> "People who love ideas must have a love of words, and that means, given a chance, they take a vivid interest in the clothes which words wear."
>
> —*Beatrice Warde*

typography

Combine content and style with lettering know-how

I have a little problem. It has to do with words and letters. I find a rubber stamp alphabet more tempting than chocolate. I lost count of my computer fonts somewhere after five thousand. I can identify certain typefaces by name on sight. I actually enjoy doing hand-cut titles. Let's face it: I'm addicted to type. A person like me could be called a type-aholic, but I prefer to think of myself as a font savant. Sounds much better, doesn't it?

Since words play a leading role alongside photos on scrapbook pages, I love to get creative when integrating text treatments, called typography, into a design. Typography encompasses the style, arrangement and appearance of lettering.

While typography is not customarily an element of design, I have treated it as such in this book since it's so crucial in scrapbook design. Because titles and journaling are at the heart of scrapbooking, it makes sense to address the impact typography plays in a layout's design alongside the traditional elements of line, shape, space, texture and color.

Even if you are not a typography junkie like I am, you will likely be using text somewhere on your next layout. While you may not place journaling on every page you create, at minimum the layout will have a title and perhaps a simple caption. Just as our words can add depth to the content of a layout, text can add another dimension to a page's design.

integrate text into the design

While we are all guilty of putting off the journaling to the very end, it pays to plan ahead. Planning out the location and length of text elements during the preliminary design results in a more unified finished result. Instead of taking text for granted or treating it like an afterthought, make sure your words are working for your design. For successful results when planning how to incorporate typography, rely on the principles of design to guide you.

Proportion, scale and emphasis: Use scale and proportion to establish the desired impact of the type among the other elements of a design. In particular, make sure the title is in scale so it can hold its own on the layout. Use emphasis to further distinguish the importance of the title in the design.

Rhythm: Look for typefaces that share the line and shape of other aspects of the design. A graphic, linear layout might look best with a contemporary sans-serif font, while an old-fashioned script will feel at home with a romantic shabby chic design.

Balance: Treat the journaling block and title component like value areas. While looking at a journaling block, squint your eyes to determine how "heavy" a text area feels. Seeing text as a page design element will help you decide how it affects the balance of a composition.

Unity: Choose lettering styles that are consistent with the mood and theme of the layout. Execute text in colors, textures and materials that are in agreement with the design as a whole. See pages 54–55 for tips and more information about choosing the perfect typeface styles for your layouts.

keep type reader-friendly

As a designer, you have the important job of making your text both visually appealing and reader-friendly. Journaling should be comfortable to read. Avoid too-small type by executing lettering in a minimum size of ten to twelve points (or its equivalent for handwritten journaling). Be aware that some typefaces might look great as a title but don't work well for the smaller, continuous text of journaling. In such cases, pick a legible journaling typeface that complements the title font. Your words should have enough contrast between the lettering and background colors to show up well. For instance, black lettering on a red background can be hard to read since the two colors are close in value. Also assess the legibility of text over patterns. Handwritten journaling should be straight and orderly, with clear letter shapes and tidy execution.

For titles, think through the same criteria to check for readability. The title should stand out against the background. If the title does not feel distinctive, try matting the letters in a contrasting color, inking the edges for definition, popping the letters off the page with foam adhesive or placing the title on a backdrop that will garner it more distinction, such as a tag or paper strip. Make sure multiple words in a title read in a logical manner. We naturally read from left to right and top to bottom. Check that the eye can string the words together in a natural way. If the title has an unconventional direction, such as vertical orientation, it is even more important that the letters themselves are clear and visually connected.

get creative with text

Once you are comfortable with the basics of typography, you may want to try more unconventional approaches to

In this travel layout, a modern sans-serif typeface echoes the industrial feel of the pictured attraction and the circular shapes that appear throughout the design. The page title includes a touch of whimsy by replacing the O's with round clip art tags. A drop cap connects the journaling to the title and plays off the small photo. Computer journaling placed on top of the large photo makes good use of open space and creates a seamless appearance.

Supplies: Red, blue cardstocks · Patterned papers (KI Memories) · Paper tab (Autumn Leaves) · Metal rimmed acrylic tags (Club Scrap) · Yellow brads · Silver thread · Blue pen · Eye, flag clip art (www.microsoft.com) · Walkway font

In the wilderness of the back garden, Zooey steps gingerly through the fresh green grass. He first makes a circuit of the fence to check that all is as it should be in his personal jungle. Only then is it time for a bit of luxuriant relaxation. There in the corner, under the big rose bush, he seeks the perfect triangular patch of grass. It is dappled in sunlight. It is cool and refreshing. It is tall and uncut (courtesy of Tom's thoughtful lawn mowing). It is the ultimate spot to roll round upon and curl up into, resulting in a glorious kitty bird nest. True pudgy splendor!

Splendor in the Grass

In conjunction with the focal-point photo, this design is built around the illuminated letter S. The colorful accent acts as both a functional letter in the title and an eye-catching page embellishment. To create this distinctive text treatment, the cat image was stamped twice in black dye ink, first on ivory cardstock and then on sage cardstock. Watercolor paints were used to color both images. An S was cut from the sage image and mounted over the ivory version.

Supplies: Cardstocks: brown, orange (Bazzill), light green (Club Scrap) · Uptown patterned papers (Cross My Heart) · Bamboo paper (Be Unique) · Vellum (Grafix) · Cat stamp (Stamps Happen) · Angora watercolors (Canson) · Black ink pad · Nick Bantock Van Dyke brown ink (Ranger) · Sage photo corners · Green rickrack · Green thread · Foam adhesive · Skylark ITC font

the written word. Typography can lend itself to all kinds of creative formatting within a design. Who says text always should have an even baseline, be in the same color or have a horizontal placement? While there is nothing wrong with keeping it simple, feel free to work around the tried-and-true rules. As long as you maintain readability, you can bend typography conventions in endless directions to make original design statements.

In addition, consider ways in which typography can be fully integrated into a composition. Look beyond where the text will fit to how the text could best be presented, resulting in dynamic, unified designs. For example, "Splendor in the Grass" (page 49) contains an illuminated letter that acts as both an embellishment and title starter.

For inspiration, keep an eye out for typography ideas in print materials such as magazines, posters, advertisements, product labels and Web sites. Graphic designers continually come up with fresh approaches to text that you can then adapt to your own projects. In a magazine you might see a design that cleverly formats running text, and then on a trendy T-shirt you might spot a cool title treatment. The typography on "Coca-Cola Museum" below takes its cue from print material. The title treatment is akin to vintage advertisements and the journaling format was inspired by a magazine article. Sketch or place copies of the ideas that interest you in an inspiration notebook for future reference.

Make your heartfelt words an integral part of the page design by choosing coordinating lettering, utilizing the principles of design and maintaining readability. Both lettering novices and font savants can use a dose of design know-how to successfully incorporate typography onto scrapbook layouts.

After seeing a magazine article about chicken collectibles in which the text was cleverly formatted into a chicken shape, I was inspired to create a journaling block for this layout in which the text follows the distinctive contours of the famous Coke bottle. In addition, the title is reminiscent of a vintage Coca-Cola coaster or advertisement. Both typography treatments, inspired by print materials, result in text that is well-integrated into the layout's theme and design.

Supplies: White, red cardstocks · Coca-Cola patterned papers, bottle caps (EK Success) · Thread · Foam adhesive · Loki-Cola font · Devroye font

It didn't get much better on a weekend afternoon than hanging out with our gang in the park. While our parents did their own hanging out, we kids would play on the swings and jungle gym or have games of tag and hide-and-seek. We were an assortment of ages ranging from little Melinda at two to Jessica at ten, but it didn't seem to matter to us. We could happily play and pretend together for hours! Acton, Massachusetts ~ July 1979

For the typography on this layout documenting a 1970s memory in retro style, it was appropriate to choose typefaces with corresponding retro character. The hand-cut title employs a font with some of the groovy traits typical of type of that era: a curvy silhouette, a bottom-heavy shape and a left-leaning tilt. Since this type would be hard to read in a small point size, a coordinating font was chosen for the journaling. For more about selecting coordinating typefaces, see page 54.

PHOTO: CHRIS PUBLOW
JOURNALING: JESSIE BALDWIN

Supplies: Avocado green cardstock · Solid rust, solid yellow, patterned papers (Chatterbox) · Wooden beads · Eyelets · Jute rickrack · Twine · Really Rust dye ink pad (Stampin' Up!) · Wavy decorative scissors (Craft Cut) · Clear thread · Daisy punch · Foam adhesive · Backhand Brush font · Pine Casual font

top-notch titles

Create maximum impact with these eye-catching title techniques:

substitute a letter with image
Add a touch of whimsy by replacing a letter or two in the title words with an embellishment. Just be sure to maintain legibility.

pop off the page
Give a title distinction against a busy background by placing it within a tag or border.

go multi-media
Mix lettering made from a variety of materials for playful effects and interesting textural variations.

repeat for emphasis
Duplicate a title multiple times in different text treatments to create dynamic word play. Stagger, stack or place them around the design in creative locations.

shake up case and orientation
Rather than confining your title lettering to the traditional upper and lower case order, mix the cases in nontraditional ways. For a twist, turn a letter in an unexpected direction.

experiment with placement
Think outside tried-and-true convention that says titles should run horizontally and be at the top of a page. Instead, try placing the title vertically or diagonally, in another spot besides the top left corner.

play favorites
Break up the monotony of uniform lettering by highlighting particular letters in the title. Emphasize the initial letters of major words or pick random letters within. Add spunk to chosen letters by changing the color or size, matting them or varying height with foam adhesive.

Supplies: Celery, purple, white, red cardstocks · Patterned papers: Walter Knabe blue designs (Paper Adventures), green designs (Anna Griffin), purple designs (Karen Foster Design), black swirl (Rusty Pickle), red polka dot (Heart & Home), red berry (Magenta), green check · Letter brads (Colorbök)· Chipboard letter X (Basic Grey) · Acrylic tile letters: red round (Junkitz), black square (Doodlebug Design) · Woven letter M (Scrapworks) · Snowflake charm, silver brad, button, green metal letter S, chipboard letter A (Making Memories) · Jolee's vellum snowflakes (EK Success) · Flower punch · Black brads · Ribbon · Thread · Acrylic paint · Foam adhesive · Computer fonts

jazzy journaling

Add some sparkle to your prose with these ideas for journaling elements:

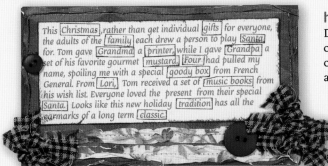

highlight for emphasis

Differentiate words within a journaling block by accenting certain words with chalk, changing font color, coating with crystal lacquer or by creating a cut-and-paste look with blocks of a different paper.

integrate title and text block

Start your journaling with a drop cap (a larger first letter) or an illuminated letter that echoes the title lettering to create continuity between the title and journaling.

apply form and function

Ground a journaling block to other aspects of a design by formatting its text on a contained unit like a tag, mini file folder or library pocket.

capitalize on an open spot

Add journaling to an open space on a photo using image-editing software, a transparency or an opaque pen.

offer design support

Add supporting information on tabs, label holders, tags or other small embellishments to mix up the shapes and textures of the text.

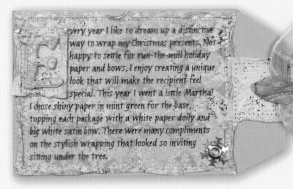

mix it up

Combine handwriting with computer fonts or lettering products for contrast and a change of pace. Even a small bit of hand-writing can add an appealing personal touch.

connect the elements

Make a visual bond from the photos to the words by connecting them with embellishments. For example, hang the journaling block from the focal-point photo with jump rings, tied ribbons or hinges.

Supplies: Rust, celery, chartreuse, cream, purple cardstocks · Patterned papers: red floral (Anna Griffin), red harlequin (K & Company), dark green stripe and dots, Walter Knabe light green and blue designs (Paper Adventures) · Transparency (Grafix) · Tiny tag (American Tag Company) · White label holder, buttons (Making Memories) · Gingham fabric · Snowflake eyelet · Thread · Ribbon · Purple, rust, olive dye inks · Le Plume olive green pen (Marvy) · Wavy decorative scissors (Craft Cut) · Computer fonts

the right type

When you begin to make decisions about how to best integrate text into a design, an important step is to choose the right style of lettering. All kinds of lettering, from letter stickers to alphabet brads to computer fonts, are based upon a typeface. A typeface is the style or design of a set of coordinating letters and/or numbers. After viewing thousands of pages submitted by readers to *Memory Makers* magazine during my tenure as craft editor, I have identified the following as the three basic challenges scrapbook designers face when choosing typefaces.

Challenge #1
Choosing a typeface that fits a layout's theme or mood

Typefaces have distinct personalities, so your goal is to find some that will feel right at home with the message of your layout. Is it formal or casual? Feminine or masculine? Modern or old-fashioned? Sedate or lively? Train your eye to see the character of the type. This is not an exact science, of course, but by applying descriptive words you are bound to find an appropriate choice that will suit your design. I utilize font management software to keep track of my own font collection. I have found it very useful to cross-reference my fonts into categories, including typeface kind (typewriter, script, handwriting, etc.), historical style (Art Deco, 1960s, Gothic), and mood or theme (elegant, feminine, urban). When I am looking for a font, I simply go to a collection that fits my design's message.

elegant & feminine
Aa Bb Cc Dd

whimsical & old world
Aa Bb Cc Dd

casual & playful
Aa Bb Cc Dd

urban & masculine
Aa Bb Cc Dd

Challenge #2
Choosing typeface pairs for coordinating title and journaling sets

A typeface that looks great as a title may not be the best choice for running text, and vice versa. It usually works best to select the title typeface first and then pick a journaling type to go with it. Choose a title typeface based on the

ABCDEFG
AaBbCcDd

ABCD
AaBbCcDd

ABCDEFG
AaBbCcDd

layout's theme or mood; then use those same adjectives to pick a simple, easy-to-read journaling font. In addition, you will want the set to have similar structural characteristics. Consider traits such as line quality, serif style, the shape

of extenders, commonality of form for distinct letters such as "a" and "g," and the height, width and direction of the letters. You will probably not be able to find two fonts that share all these traits, so look for a pair that has enough in common that they go together well.

Challenge #3
Choosing multiple typefaces for titles

Creative typography design can include titles made up of several different typefaces, as long as there is a harmonious contrast. For the sake of design unity, the typefaces should work together even while they contrast. For example, the combination of a handwriting-like font and an inky typewriter-like font that shares an old-fashioned aesthetic will most likely be successful, while an Art Deco serif mixed with a sci-fi style serif probably will not. As a rule of thumb, don't use more than three different typefaces in one design.

back to
SCHOOL
August 27, 2007

Grandma's Little
SWEETHEART
sarah elizabeth

typeface traits defined

When you are looking at distinctions from one typeface to the next, be aware of the components of lettering that define each unique typeface.

bowl: the round element of a letter

ascender: the stroke that extends above the bowl of a letter shape

descender: the stroke that extends below the baseline or bowl of a letter shape

serif: tiny marks on the end of a letter that finish off the stroke; if a typeface is sans serif, it does not contain such marks

finial: the decoration or flourish at the end of a stroke, such as a teardrop or hook

flourish: a stroke added to a letter for style rather than meaning

oblique: a slanted version of a typeface; italics are right-slanted obliques

baseline: the imaginary line that letter shapes sit upon

tracking: the space between letters in a typeface, similar to kerning

kerning: the space between specific letters

leading: the space between lines of text

point size (pica): the measurement of type size

serif

sans-serif

finials

flourishes

letter shapes

Just like handwriting varies from person to person, each typeface is unique. Letter shapes can differ greatly from one typeface to another. The shape of individual letters is dependant on how its bowl, ascenders and descenders are executed, along with any stylistic elements, such as serifs, finials or flourishes it may contain. It is these shapes along with the line quality that give a typeface its personality.

Some letters have greater variations from one typeface to another, such as a, g, y, A, K and Q. Look at the character of these letters in particular when you are choosing coordinating font pairs. Also pay close attention to a particular letter if it will be the first letter of your title.

OLIVE COMF_EXIC

Yellow ocher, rose doré + white

Yellow ocher + white

SHADOWS

SHADOWS

Cerulean
blue +
cadmium r...

Cadmium
red + raw

Raw sienna
+ cobalt
blue

Permanent
mauve

Cadmium red
+ cobalt blue

Alizarin
crimson +
raw umber

HIGHLIGHTS

Naples
yellow

color

3

...at

technique are still used today. For t...
best results, the colors must be close...
in tone (i.e. of a similar lightness o...
darkness). Here are some exam...
you may need to hold the boo...
...m you so that the "optical...
...ke place.

White

Purple

Green

12
MALKREIDEN
CRAIES

12
Craies

These eyes are known to sparkle with mirth and mischief, an expression of their curious, intelligent owner. These eyes change shades of blue to reflect her mood or color of clothing, just like her daddy's eyes do. These eyes see everyone she meets as a potential friend and every situation as a chance to play or explore. Behind these eyes is an observant fouryear old that wants to understand how the world works; a little girl who is mostly sweet and sometimes sassy. They belong to none other than our darling Kendall, with eyes so bright and blue!

bright&blue

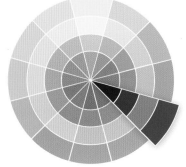

March 17 2006

Inspired by the subject's bright eyes and clothing, a refreshing blue and white color scheme was chosen for this layout. Blues in various values and intensities create a monochromatic color scheme that is anything but monotonous.

PHOTOS: MICHELLE PESCE

Supplies: White cardstock (Prism Papers) · Blue cardstock · Patterned papers: turquoise floral, light blue paisley (Sandylion), blue swirl (KI Memories), dark blue abstract (Anna Griffin)· Butterfly stamp (Hero Arts) · Paint chip · Brocade Blue dye ink (Stampin' Up!) · Ribbon · Paper flowers (Prima) · Buttons · Corner rounder (EK Success) · Thread · Foam adhesive (3L) · SouciSans font

color theory

Explore color theory with classic color-wheel combinations

a s a scrapbook artist, what do you have most in common with master painters like Vermeer, van Gogh and Matisse? The answer: Color! No matter what the medium, color is the most powerful element in a designer's tool box. Since it is the first element a viewer notices in a design, color has the ability to express emotion and mood in a very direct manner. Color is one of the most important aspects of design that you can master. Color is such an important element of design that it merits its own section. By giving color lots of room in this book, we are able to study several aspects of its complex character. This first section covers color theory and traditional color schemes. It includes a color wheel and many examples to inspire you. The next section goes a bit deeper to discuss color value. The third section talks about the fascinating concept of color language. Lastly, the color palettes section compares how different sets of color choices can affect a design.

A great way to start exploring color theory is by putting classic color schemes into practice on your pages. Through decades of experimentation, artists have established tried-and-true color schemes based on the color wheel. Understanding these color schemes can be invaluable as you plan pages. The harmonies and contrasts built into these color schemes will take out the guesswork and help unify a design. But even though these color combinations have

structure, they can look different every time you use them. You can interpret each one in a personal way, choosing the value, intensity and temperature for each color. The more you practice combining colors within the established schemes, the further you will develop your own color intuition.

the color wheel

As we look at color combinations, use the color wheel on page 62 as a guide. A color wheel is a visual aid for understanding how colors work together. Note that the word color is interchangeable with the term hue.

The color wheel is divided into four rings. The outermost ring consists of colors in their purest form. The inside rings contain variations of those pure colors.

The colors on the outside ring of the wheel fall into one of three categories: primary, secondary or tertiary. Red, blue and yellow are primary colors. They are pure, having no other colors in them. These three colors are the foundation for the entire color wheel; all other colors are mixed from the primaries.

On the wheel, the primary colors are spaced equally apart and form a triangle. The secondary colors occupy the locations that exist halfway between each of the primaries; they are green, orange and purple. A secondary color is a mixture of the two primary colors on each adjacent side.

Filling in every other space is a tertiary color. A tertiary is made by mixing a primary and a secondary color. The resulting color names reflect their make-up and position, such as purple-red.

properties of color

Before we look at color schemes, let's first go over the properties of color. When you pick a color scheme, you will often use variations of its pure colors, such as pink instead of red. The variations exist because of shifts in the pure color's properties—value, intensity and temperature.

Value is the lightness or darkness of a color. A high value is called a tint and is created by adding white to a pure color. A low value is called a shade and is made by adding black to a pure color. Variations in value add visual interest because they create contrast.

Intensity is the brightness of a color. Changing the value of a color by adding white or black will also affect its intensity. To lower the intensity of a light or bright color, add gray. The result is called a tone. Pure, bright colors have the highest intensity while colors with black or gray have the lowest. The intensity of a color affects its mood and emphasis in a design.

Temperature is the warmth or coolness of a color. In basic terms, red, orange and yellow are warm colors and relate to blood, fire and sun. Blue, green and purple are cool colors; they relate to water, plant life and night, respectively. Temperature can create depth, movement and mood.

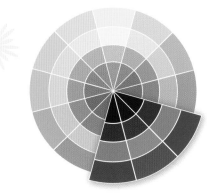

A patchwork of patterned papers in an analogous color scheme of blue, blue-purple and purple create a cool, crisp backdrop for a wintry photo. The understated color variations create a subtle, serene mood.

PHOTO: ALLISON ORTHNER

Supplies: White cardstock · Matte metallic silver cardstock (Club Scrap) · Patterned papers: Sarah Bond watercolor designs (Autumn Leaves), purple snowflake (Karen Foster Designs) · White felt · Glass seed beads · Silver thread (Sulky) · Transparency · White embossing powder (Stampendous!) · Foam adhesive · Le Plume purple pen (Marvy) · Viner Hand ITC font

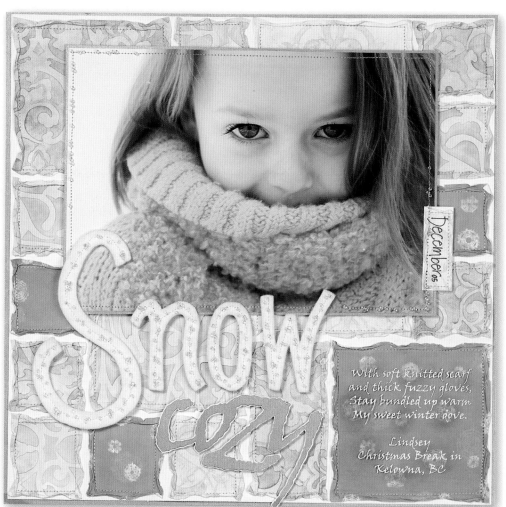

a Love Letter to

Preston

Precious Preston,
You are such a sweet and precious baby boy with your big beautiful hazel eyes that seem almost green at times. Your sweet smile which always seems readily available for those who choose to talk to you is so endearing. Rocking you in the little rocker in your lovely little boy bedroom is a delight beyond compare. I can close my eyes and revel in the moment of closeness along with the sweet baby smell that is all yours. Watching you push up on your little back legs starting to crawl and reach up to things is a thrill that only loved ones get to enjoy. Watching big brother Oliver giving you lots of hugs and kisses, and the sparkle in your eyes tells us that you adore him as well. God gave us a truly great gift when he gave us our baby boy Preston to love and adore.

Great Grandma Irene

In addition to containing a special letter to Preston from his great-grandmother, this layout also employs a triadic color scheme. Its three main colors of red, blue, and yellow form a triangle on the color wheel. While the pure hues contrast off each other, the color scheme is harmonious because they are used in different quantities.

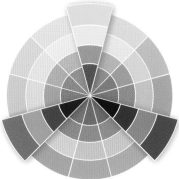

Supplies: Red, cream cardstocks (Bazzill) · Patterned papers: Melissa Frances polka dot (Heart & Home), yellow check (Anna Griffin), blue quilt (Memories Complete) · Toys cut from wrapping paper (Cavallini Papers & Co.) · Transparency (Grafix) · Brown ink pad (Stampin' Up!) · Red buttons · All Night Media foam adhesive (Plaid) · Red thread · Computer fonts

the color wheel

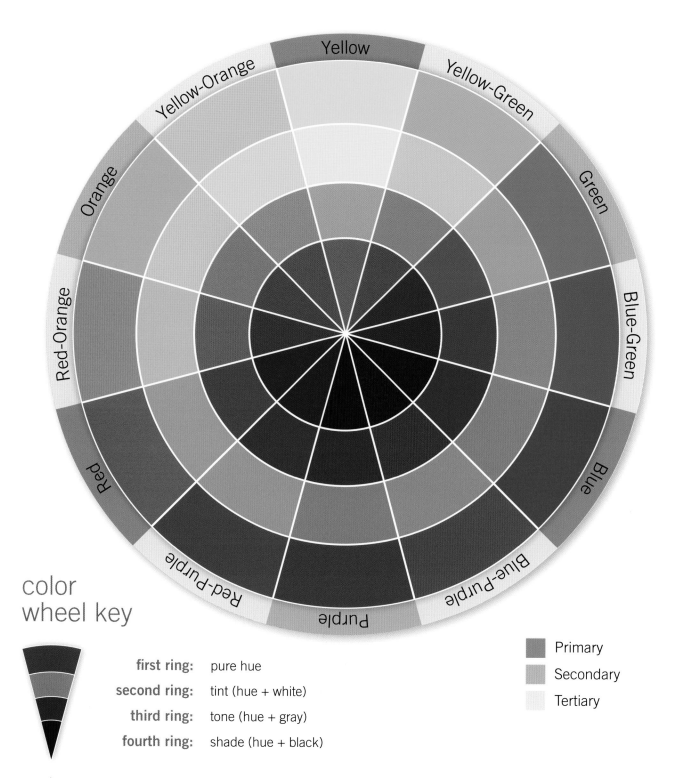

color wheel key

first ring:	pure hue
second ring:	tint (hue + white)
third ring:	tone (hue + gray)
fourth ring:	shade (hue + black)

Primary
Secondary
Tertiary

color recipes

The variations of a pure color result from how it is mixed. Here are the color formulas:

tint = hue + white

shade = hue + black

tone = hue + gray

white   tint

pure hue   gray   tone

black   shade

properties of color

Each variation of a hue has its own properties of value, intensity and temperature. This chart shows how such properties graduate outward from the pure colors in the center.

intensity

value

value = lightness or darkness of a color

intensity = brightness or dullness of a color

temperature = warmth or coolness of a color

cool colors   warm colors

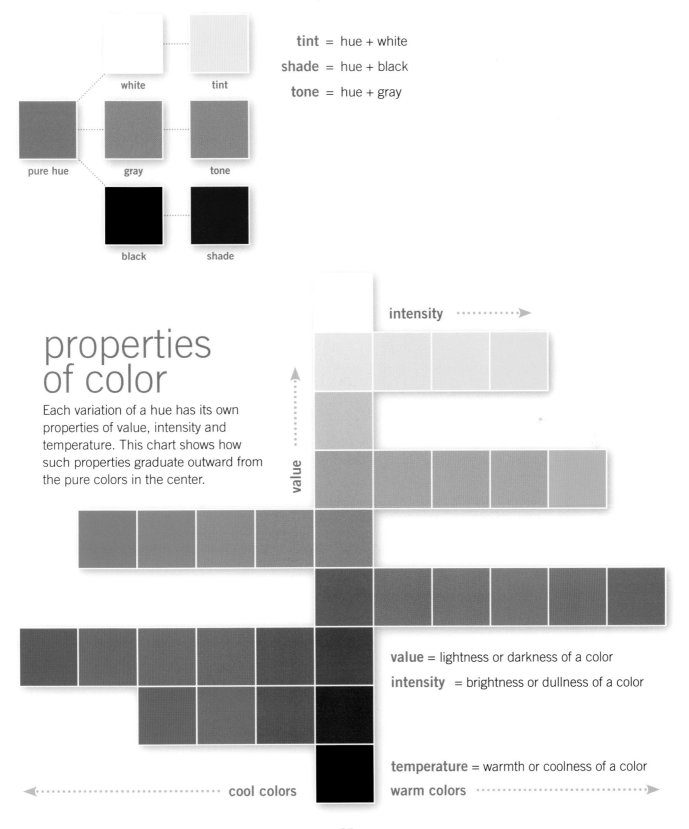

On the color wheel, red-orange is the warmest color and green-blue is the coolest. As colors radiate in either direction from red-orange, they will become cooler. Therefore, an individual color will be warmer or cooler depending on its proximity to either red-orange or green-blue.

Note that there are both warm and cool variations of each color on the color wheel. If you have ever been on a mission to find the perfect red lipstick, you have encountered this subtle aspect of color temperature at work. After trying on a handful of lipsticks, it becomes clear that reds are not all the same: some are warmer (with a yellow tinge), while others are cooler (with a blue

tinge). The right one for you depends on whether your complexion has warm or cool undertones. This same concept is at play with colors in design. When colors clash, it is likely due to mixing individual hues with different temperatures.

the classic color schemes

The character of each color scheme is based on either similarity or contrast. Combinations with similar variations, such as monochromatic and analogous, are understated and refined, and often the easiest to execute. **Monochromatic** color schemes consist of just one color;

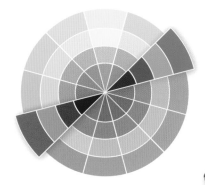

A childhood portrait of my mother and uncle looks right at home with a border of vintage illustrations. The storybook images were distressed for an aged effect and then placed against a complementary color scheme of red and green.

Supplies: Red, green, pink, ivory cardstocks · Patterned papers: green plaid (Provo Craft), red plaid (Making Memories), Brenda Walton light green floral (K & Company), dark green floral (Anna Griffin) · Vintage illustrations (Vintage Workshop) · Nick Bantock charcoal gray ink (Ranger) · Pearl buttons · Ribbon (Offray) · Thread · Foam adhesive · Chalk · Oz Handicraft BT font

Connie's Bubby

Connie and little brother Galen were inseparable playmates. Only 16 months apart, they happily invented games together, slept in matching bunk beds, loved to hear stories, and played outside with the neighbor kids. Connie always looked out for Galen, even after they started in school. Galen liked to do everything she did, even copying things she said. He would say to his mother, "Connie wants a drink", when he wanted a drink for himself, mimicking the way he had heard his sissy ask. Connie had trouble saying Galen's name, so from the word brother, "Bubby" became her name for him. Galen continued to be called Bubby by all who knew him as late as when he started high school.

1946
Twin Falls, Idaho

• Our Impish Photo Shoot •

I had the camera and backdrop all set up and was hoping to get a decent shot of Connor for our family Christmas card, but I didn't really have high hopes that he would cooperate. He wasn't even dressed yet when to my surprise, he picked up a Santa hat and seemed happy to wear it. I hastily pulled a red shirt over Connor's head and we started taking pictures. Things quickly went downhill as Connor burst into tears, Alvin had trouble working the camera, and I became increasingly desperate to get The Perfect Photo. Before long, Connor and I were both in tears, Alvin was mad, and we gave up completely.

About half an hour later, Connor shocked me by walking in with the Santa hat and sitting in the chair in front of the backdrop. I handed him a candy cane and was lucky to finally catch some festive shots of our little elf! Then he shared his candy cane with me, and Alvin got some cute ones of Connor and me together, too. It was traumatic, but in the end we got our Christmas card photo and more! 12.03

Little Elf

Elf Connor's
Christmas Wish List

- a puppy
- a slide
- trucks & cars
- Hokey Pokey Elmo

A double complementary color scheme of red/green and purple/yellow is nice rather than naughty on this Christmas layout. While red is the dominant color, splashes of purple and yellow bring a fresh twist to the traditional holiday color scheme. To add to the festive mood, candy cane accents were fashioned out of air-dry clay.

PHOTOS AND JOURNALING: SUSAN CYRUS

Supplies: White, purple cardstocks · Patterned papers: red dot (Printworks), green diamond (Scrapbook Wizard) · Photo corners (Canson) · All Night Media Mary Engelbreit stamps (Plaid) · Black dye ink · Purple pigment ink · Angora watercolors (Canson) · Colored pencils · Ribbon · Silver eyelets (Making Memories) · Silver snowflake eyelet · Makin's clay in red and white (Provo Craft) · Buttons · Thread · Foam adhesive · Addict font · BlackJack font

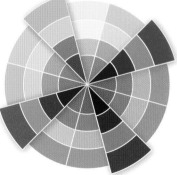

interest is created by varying the values and intensities. An example would be using red, pink, rose and burgundy on a layout. "Bright & Blue" (page 58) demonstrates a successful monochromatic color scheme.

Analogous color schemes use colors next to each other on the color wheel. They are pleasing because of their interesting yet low-key gradations. While based on similarities, analogous color schemes provide an understated zing. The layout "Snow Cozy" (page 60) shows a wintry analogous combination of blue, blue-purple and purple.

Triadic and complemenatary color schemes work because of color contrast, producing dynamic interplays of color on layouts.

Triadic schemes consist of three colors that are equidistant on the color wheel, forming a triangle. For the best results, use the three colors in different amounts. "A Love Letter to Preston," on page 61, uses a basic primary triad of red, yellow and blue for a playful effect.

Complementary colors, such as blue and orange or purple and yellow, reside directly across from each other on the wheel. As one color is cool and the other warm, their contrast creates a spirited result. Choose one color to be dominant. Because of the high contrast, it can confuse the eye if the two complementary colors are shown in equal measure. Red and green make up the complementary color scheme used on "Connie's Bubby" on page 64.

Double-complementary schemes are made up of four colors that are two sets of complementary colors. On the wheel, the sets form a square or rectangle. Choose one dominant color for the design, with the other three in smaller, but not necessarily equal ratios. "Little Elf" on page 65 employs the complementary pairs of red/green and purple/yellow. Red is the prominent color in the design, with various doses of the other three colors throughout.

Split-complementary schemes consist of three colors—one color and the two colors on each side of its complement (forming a "Y" on the color wheel). Again, it's best to pick one color for dominance and use the others as accents. On "Winter," shown on the opposite page, green-blue is foremost, accented by tints of red and orange.

Utilize the classic color schemes in order to choose harmonious combinations that best suit each scrapbook design. Once you practice using these color schemes, you can grow beyond them to find your own distinct color expressions.

When we moved to Minnesota, I would have never guessed that Abby would love winter so much! Having snowball fights with Ryan or hurling down the slide into a huge pile of snow are perfect ways to expend that cabin fever energy she can amass. Abby takes joy in marking our yard with snow angels, which result in an amazing amount of giggles. This winter there was enough snow for Abby and Ryan to make a grand, old-fashioned snowman with a jaunty scarf and a real carrot nose. They were very proud of their new friend! Abby's newest wintertime activity is to create snow art, made by spraying the snow with colored water. Now our snow comes in green, pink and blue as well as white. But most of all, I love to watch Abby enjoy the quiet winter moments, like trying to catch snowflakes on her tongue or taking a taste out of a snowball, after which she declared "I love to eat snow!" ~~Winter 2004

Neutral white works in tandem with a split complementary color scheme in blue-green, red and orange to create a winter wonderland with a joyful mood. The colors are unified by their cool color temperature even while the blue contrasts against the tints of red and orange. White acrylic paint was liberally applied throughout the layout to create a snowy effect.

PHOTOS AND JOURNALING: PAULA DEREAMER

Supplies: Teal, peach, white cardstocks · Pink paper, striped pink paper (Chatterbox) · Transparency (Grafix) · Paper Plus crackle finish (Delta) · Acrylic paint · Paper slide mounts (Design Originals) · Winter is Calling stamp set (Stampin' Up!) · Metal moulding strips, photo corners, word plaques, decorative brads (Making Memories) · Angora watercolors (Canson) · Black dye ink · Fiber (FoofaLa) · White glitter (Sulyn Industries) · Colored pencils · Foam adhesive · Effloresce Antique font

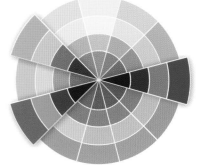

6 classic color schemes defined

Follow these examples to pick tried-and-true color combinations.

monochromatic

different values of a single color

analogous

colors adjacent to each
other on the color wheel

triadic

three colors equidistant from
each other on the color wheel

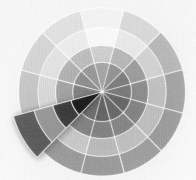

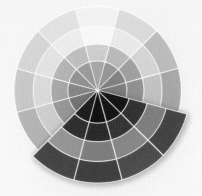

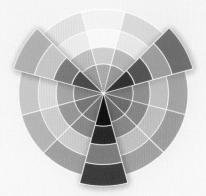

Supplies for all tags: Various colored cardstocks · Silver crinkle paper · Patterned papers (Deluxe Designs, Design Originals, EK Success, Frances Meyer, Hot Off The Press, Scrapbook Wizard, Treehouse Designs) · Stamps: star, bunnies (Stampendous!), Hep Santa (JudiKins), small ornaments (DeNami Design), large ornament (Plaid), Jone Hallmark Santa and angel (PrintWorks) · Twinkling H_2O paints (LuminArte) · Silver pigment ink · Silver ultra fine embossing powder (Stamp A Mania) · Rhinestones (Me & My Big Ideas) · Silver glitter/micro bead mix (Rubba Dub Dub) · Silver floss · Ribbon · Woven labels (Making Memories, Me & My Big Ideas) · Rub-ons, buttons (Making Memories) · Eyelets · Foam adhesive

complementary

two colors directly opposite one
another on the color wheel

**double
complementary**

two pairs of complementary
colors, situated on the color wheel
to form a square or rectangle

**split-
complementary**

three colors—one color plus
the two colors on either
side of its complement

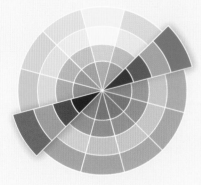
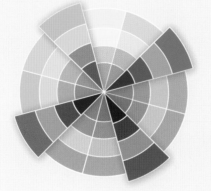
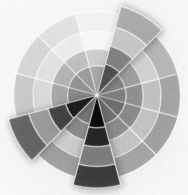

music to go

april 06

My iPod is truly a wonder to be treasured. I love its small size and sleek design, making it a cinch to take with me almost everywhere I go. This compact device holds all my favorite songs in one handy, easy-to-use place. I can put music on it from a variety of sources, such as: download an entire CD that I already own or go to the iTunes website to buy just a single song that I want. iTunes makes it easy to hear and purchase the latest music as it comes out. The iPod is one of those brilliant inventions that makes you wonder what you did without it!

Here is a sampling of some current favorites from my iPod playlist for April 2006:

Vienna * Billy Joel
Somewhere Only We Know * Keane
Blue Orchid * The White Stripes
Ride * The Vines
Summon You * Spoon

Do You Want To * Franz Ferdinand
It Wasn't Me * Jenny Lewis & the Watson Twins
The WAND * The Flaming Lips
Bar Star * Kudu

my favorites

f

treats

april 06

...ems I am among a rare few that are not chocoholics. I like chocolate, but would rather have caramel or coffee flavors! My favorite treats reflect that preference. For an indulgence, I crave ice cream the most. My favorite picks are rich, creamy Dulce de Leche and Caramel Cone from Haagen-Dazs. It's a good thing they only come in those little cartons! For a more everyday treat, my car heads right to Starbucks. My usual: a venti sugar-free hazelnut latte, please! The hazelnut syrup adds a caramelly, graham cracker flavor to the dark roasted and frothy coffee drink. Can't beat that combination!

color

march 06

I love color! Though I was cautious about color when I was younger, it is now a prominent part of my life. In general I like all colors, depending on their hue and context, but I find myself particularly drawn to red, pink, purple and green. It is interesting that the first three are directly related, since red is the base for both pink and purple. This green-eyed girl finds green calm and refreshing. It is a color I often treat as a neutral since to me it goes with everything. I love crisp green so much that I named my business after that color! Red, pink, purple and green are prevalent in all aspects of my life, including my wardrobe, home decor and artwork.

This 8 x 8" (20cm x 20cm) mini album featuring a few of my favorite things uses vibrant colors as a unifying design factor throughout its pages. The high-value, high-intensity hues found in the stamped accents and paper flowers create a funky, energetic mood.

Supplies: 8 x 8" album (Mara-Mi) · Purple cardstock (Bazzill) · White cardstock · Patterned paper (Paper Fever) · Stamps (Paula Best) · Nick Bantock Van Dyke brown dye ink (Ranger) · Angora watercolors (Canson) · Purple fabrics · Gingham ribbon · Purple thread · Brads (Die Cuts With A View) · Flowers (Prima) · Index tabs · Le Plume purple pen (Marvy) · Foam adhesive (3L) · Heat N Bond Lite iron-on fabric adhesive (Therm O Web) · My Own Topher font

value

Understand the factors beneath a color scheme

If I hadn't become an avid scrapbooker, it is likely that I would have become a quilter. The two crafts share several appealing aspects. Both allow you to mix patterns in eye-pleasing combinations, are tactile creative outlets, and have lovely supplies. The supplies are so nice, in fact, that I have many of them even though I have yet to make a quilt. One of the cool quilting tools I have is called a value viewer. This device consists of two colored transparent films, one green and one red, each housed in a cardboard frame. When you view a fabric using the films, you no longer see the fabric's color but instead can clearly see its value—the lightness or darkness of a color. Sounds nifty, but how does this help a quilter?

A quilt consists of colored fabrics arranged into a geometric design. But even more important than the colors of the fabrics used, a successful quilt depends on the value of those colors. It is the arrangement of light, medium and dark values that truly builds the quilt's design and gives it definition and dimension. Quilters can use a value viewer to assist in determining a fabric's value, which in turn helps them choose the best fabric combination for their design.

While value does not play such a front-and-center role for scrapbook pages, it is still important in a behind-the-scenes way. Value qualities impact a layout's color scheme, which in turn affects other aspects of the design. Because

of this, a scrapbook artist, like a quilter, will benefit from an understanding of value.

Consider the color red, for example. Pink is created by adding white to red, while burgundy is created by adding black. Both colors are values of red, but the amount of white or black added changes its look and feel significantly. Remember from the previous section that a tint is created by adding white to a pure color. A tint, such as pink, is a high value. A shade is made by adding black to a pure color. A shade, like burgundy, is a low value.

Because colors are so eye-catching, it can be a challenge to see beyond a color and determine its underlying value. It helps to see value if you picture full-color designs as if they were achromatic (only black and white). Use the guide on page 72 to compare a gray value scale to a color value scale. Starting from the middle and going out, the steps of both scales get lighter as more white is added on one side, and darker as black is added on the other. With practice, or even with the assistance of a value viewer tool, you can learn to judge value patterns in addition to surface color schemes.

value and intensity

A color's intensity correlates with that color's value. Intensity is the brightness or dullness of a color. The purer a color is, the brighter it will be, which equates to high intensity

value

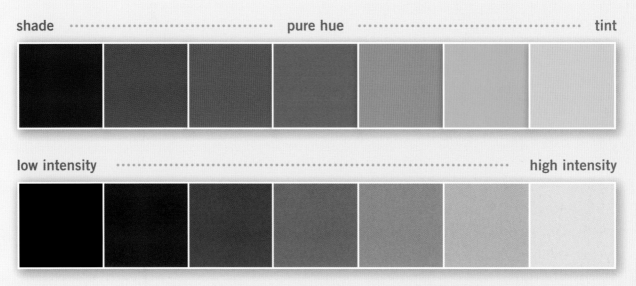

shade ·················· pure hue ·················· tint

low intensity ·················· high intensity

It's a fact that the average person can see about 40 values of a color, while those with visual acuity can see as many as 150 separate values. In a value scale, the pure hue is situated in the middle. In one direction, tints are created as white is progressively added to lighten the hue; while in the other direction, shades develop as black is added to darken the hue. The lighter the color, the higher its value. The darker the color, the lower its value.

and high value. Tones (a hue with gray added) and shades are duller and thus lower intensity. In summary, a high intensity color has a high value, while a low intensity color has a low value. Think of pure red versus brick red, which is made by mixing gray into red. When gray is added, the red's intensity diminishes and so does its value.

value and visual weight

Value contributes to a color's visual weight. The purer or lighter a color is, the less it appears to weigh. When black or gray is added, the color's value is lowered, or it gets "heavier." Let's compare pink and burgundy again. Pink is a high value color while burgundy is a low value color. If you picture equal amounts of the same color, which one seems to visually weigh more? The burgundy feels heavier because it has the lowest value of the two. In terms of page layouts, visual weight affects balance. It will take a large piece of pink cardstock to balance a small piece of burgundy. The role of visual weight will be further discussed in the Balance chapter, later in this book.

value and mood

Keep the intended mood of your design in mind when you choose not only your color scheme, but the values in the scheme. While individual colors have particular symbolic associations (we'll look at that in the next section), value can further define a color's character and contribute to the mood of a design. Dark values tend to convey a more calm and somber tone. Light values, such as brights or pastels, are more buoyant or less serious in nature. Consider the mood of the "My Favorites" mini album (page 70) with its vibrant, light-hearted brights compared to that of the mellow, low-value teals of "One Fine Day" on page 73.

The amount of contrast in values can affect its mood as well. When a design uses colors with similar values, such as peach and sage green, it feels understated, calm and subtle. When the values are far apart, as is the case with peach and black, they seem dramatic, theatrical and emotional. Whether low or high, dark or light, the contrasts in a design's value pattern affect the mood of a layout. The

I opened the door for our Sunday lunch guests, and behind the familiar faces of David and Betty Daffin was a young man. I had heard his name before, but knew nothing else until I saw him. Here was Thomas Daffin, far from home in England, quiet and reserved during this visit to his father in Texas. I myself was rather shy and insecure, but I saw this boy and knew I wanted to know him. We spent that day talking quietly to each other, the two whom otherwise were so shy. We made a certain kind of connection before the day was over, and we both knew it. It was unspoken, but we knew. If you can believe two teenagers can know such a thing. Such a fine day, such a good day to begin the correspondence of our lives.

one fine day

August 9th, 1987
Lindale, Texas

The low value quality of the colors and the overall low contrast on this layout about meeting my future husband produce an understated, dignified mood. The touches of high intensity color in the postage stamps, however, add some variety and keep the design from appearing bland.

Supplies: Light, dark teal cardstocks · Walter Knabe patterned vellum (Paper Adventures) · Postage decorative scissors (Fiskars) · Postage stamps · Fountain pen clip art · Transparencies (Grafix) · Foam adhesive · American Classic font

The color sets on these two tags both contain green and purple, but they have very different moods because of the colors' values.

Supplies: Green, white, cream cardstocks · Patterned papers: light green, purple (Anna Griffin), dark green (Frances Meyer), dark purple (C-Thru Ruler) · Tulip bouquet stamp (Stampin' Up!) · Angora watercolors (Canson) · Nick Bantock charcoal gray ink (Ranger) · Ribbon · Thread · Foam adhesive (3L)

pear cards shown below demonstrate how different the same design can look depending on its value contrast.

value and color in design

Once you understand value, you can effectively use it in conjunction with the principles that create good design—emphasis, rhythm, balance and unity. When paired with these principles of design, dynamic results are created in a layout's composition due to color's visual significance. Here's how:

Emphasis: Color can create a central focus in a layout design. By planning higher contrast in your focal-point area and subdued contrast elsewhere, you can build a place of emphasis. High-intensity colors have the most visual dominance in a design and will draw the viewer's attention first.

Rhythm: The eye will naturally follow a color or value pattern through a design. Direct this eye movement throughout the layout by repeating colors in shapes and lines. Looking at the "Alexander & the Beanstalk" layout on the opposite page, the repeated bright green papers and bean accents carry the eye around the design.

Balance: Each touch of color you add to a composition affects its balance. Look at the underlying values and determine the visual weight of each area of color. What areas of color feel lighter or heavier based on their intensity and value? Imagine the design in black and white. Are the color values balanced against each other?

Unity: Bring harmony to your layout by using close values of different colors (such as a group of pastels), or various intensities of the same color (like a monochromatic color scheme). Add a touch of variety by employing color or value contrast in a small area. A dominant color theme with accents of contrasting color is a trustworthy method for creating a unified but compelling design. For example, "One Fine Day" (page 73) utilizes high-value postage stamps to add variety to the otherwise low-value design.

Low value contrast, as shown on the left card, can create a soft, understated feel. Compare that effect to the striking, dramatic statement made by the high value contrast card shown on the right.

Supplies: Black, light chartreuse, avocado, white, cream cardstocks · Italian floral paper · Black polka dot paper (Making Memories) · Pear stamp (Just For Fun Rubber Stamps) · Twinkling H₂0 paints (LuminArte) · Black, brown inks · Photo corners (3L) · Ribbon · Buttons · Thread

Once upon a time there was a little boy called Alexander who went to visit his Grandma. Grandma had a big garden with a high wall all around it. The wall kept the rabbits out so they couldn't eat the vegetables. There were cabbages, lettuces, peas and carrots, and in one corner Alexander found an especially intriguing plant. It had big green leaves with long green beans hanging amongst them. It was growing as high as he could see, up, up into the sky. Could it be a magic beanstalk?

Now Alexander's favourite story happened to be "Jack and the Beanstalk". When the Giant said "Fee, fie, fo, fum!" Alexander's eyes would go as round as saucers. And they that did now when he looked at Grandma's beanstalk. He wondered if a giant lived at the top of this beanstalk too!

Grandma had told Alexander that peas were best picked and eaten raw, right then and there in the garden, so maybe beans were too. There was only one way to find out, so, braving any lurking giants, Alexander stepped forward and picked himself one. It was juicy and crunchy and delicious, and nobody said "Fee, fie, fo, fum!"

September 2005, North Cadbury

Alexander and the Beanstalk

If you could see your layout in black and white, how would the value pattern appear? Does the arrangement of the value pattern have balance, rhythm, unity with some variety, and a clear point of emphasis? The sharp green accents against the deep blue background produce high value contrast on this page. The high intensity of the chartreuse green creates bright beats that carry the eye across the rail and around the composition. High contrast also contributes to the striking appearance of the illuminated letters.

JOURNALING: DIONE DAFFIN

Supplies: Dark blue, chartreuse green cardstocks · Patterned papers: blue (Carolee's Creations), green dot (Anna Griffin) · Ribbon (Michaels) · Thread · Balsa wood · Green acrylic paint, buttons (Making Memories) · Night of Navy dye ink (Stampin' Up!) · Foam adhesive (3L) · Gloucester Initialen font · Biblioteque font · Jorvik Informal font

Associated with fire and blood, red conveys emotions of love, passion and excitement. Shades of red create an eye-catching statement and a striking backdrop for a creative black-and-white photograph. Elegant blue-reds and tempting textures are layered together to build a dramatic atmosphere that emulates richness and strength.

PHOTO: JENNIFER BOOTHE HATCH

Supplies: Red cardstock · Patterned papers: red design (K & Company), red floral (Basic Grey), black print, red gingham (Rusty Pickle) · Red toile tissue paper (DMD) · Vellum (Grafix) · Wooden letter "K" (Michaels) · Ribbon (Michaels, Offray, Renaissance) · Metal roses (Artchix Studio) · Red tags · Photo corners (Canson) · Red corduroy buttons (Junkitz) · Large red button · Laminate chip · Brown dye ink · Black pen · Red thread · Foam adhesive · Camilla font · Verona font

color language

Support layout themes with color connotations

have you ever wondered why the ribbon tied 'round the old oak tree is yellow? Or why red is always coupled with Valentine's Day? The answers can be found in the language of color. Every color has its own connotation, the way it makes us feel when we look at it. Our reaction to color is based on emotion and is so powerful that color can actually affect heartbeat and respiration. Because color attributes parallel how they appear in nature, most cultures associate color in comparable ways. For instance, yellow has characteristics of the sun, such as energy and hope. Red relates to blood and the heart, thus its connection to love and passion. While there can be slight variations, the associations of color are surprisingly similar around the world.

As a scrapbook artist, you can use color connections to make the same kind of emotive statements on your pages. By listening to how colors "talk," you can make more effective color choices when designing layouts.

warm colors

The warm side of the color spectrum includes red, orange and yellow. Overall, warm colors are seen as exciting, stimulating and having heat. In a design, they visually advance toward the viewer and attract immediate attention.

Red: Because of its connection to life-forces such as blood and fire, red can evoke the strongest emotions of any color. Red can raise blood pressure and increase eye blinking. It attracts more attention than other colors because it has the strongest light wavelength. It evokes feelings of passion, love, courage and power. Red is daring, intense and never subtle.

Orange: This color symbolizes the radiant glow of the sun and calls forth citrus, with its tangy, juicy flavor. In orange, the passion of red is tempered with the sunny disposition of yellow to produce a color that is bold, vibrant and energetic. Its warmth evokes spicy, tropical sensations and a gregarious, fun-loving attitude. The exuberant personality of orange is usually considered cheerful and positive, as it is born from the radiance of the eternal sun.

Yellow: Also associated with the golden light of the sun, yellow has a more purely optimistic and happy disposition than orange. As the sun will rise each day, yellow has come to symbolize hope in many cultures. Yellow ribbons worn on lapels or tied around trees in support of troops abroad are contemporary examples. In other cultures, the ties of yellow to the glorious sun and precious gold have resulted in feelings of royalty and nobility. Overall, yellow is felt to be cheerful, buoyant and outgoing.

cool colors

Green, blue and purple make up the cool side of the color palette. These colors have a cooling nature and suggest feelings of peace and restfulness. In design, cool colors recede from the viewer.

Green: More prevalent on our planet than any other color, green is abundant in nature. Because of its association with plant life, green connotes renewal, freshness and fertility. While shades of green make up the largest color family we can see, it is also the most restful color to the human eye and can slow pulse rate. With a positive association across all cultures, the natural plenitude of green symbolizes growth, harmony, balance and prosperity.

Blue: From the endless expanse of the sky to the constancy of water in lakes and oceans, blue surrounds us. Blue's ties to the sky denote a sense of serenity and spirituality. Blue's water connection evokes feelings of refreshment, cleansing and coolness. While it can also be introspective and melancholy, as in "having the blues," in general, blue is considered loyal and trustworthy, like the saying "true blue." Blue is tranquil, ethereal and refreshing.

Purple: Claude Monet said of purple, "I have finally discovered the color of the atmosphere." Like the atmosphere, ambiguous purple produces feelings of mystery, magic, contemplation and enchantment. The opulence of amethyst and the rarity of purple dye in ancient times have created purple's association with royalty, wealth, refinement and splendor. The combination of the passion of red with the serenity of blue results in the most complex of colors, and one that elicits the strongest emotional response in the cool color set.

neutrals

Although neutrals can be defined as lacking in color, they nonetheless have integral color associations of their own. Use versatile neutrals by themselves, with one other or any other color in the spectrum.

Vibrant orange and yellow create a layout mood as spirited as the page's subject. These warm colors, akin to sunshine and citrus, are undeniably energetic and upbeat.

PHOTOS: MICHELLE PESCE
JOURNALING: JENNIFER MICHAELSEN

Supplies: Orange, yellow cardstocks (Prism Papers) · Patterned papers: light and dark orange florals (Chatterbox), yellow polka dot · Paper flowers (Making Memories, Prima) · Buttons · Thread · Foam adhesive (3L) · Black Jack font

The cool color palette of purple, periwinkle, pale blue and silver gray expresses feelings of tranquility, mystery and reflection. These qualities correspond well with the water, glass and metal of the layout's subject and contribute to the serene mood of the page.

Supplies: Time & Space cardstocks, vellum (Club Scrap) · Williamsburg acrylic letter stamps (Technique Tuesday) · Stamps: harlequin (Hampton Art Stamps), florals (Magenta), asterisk, star (Hero Arts) · Pigment inks (Clearsnap, Plaid, Tsukineko) · Dye inks (Stampin' Up!) · Ribbon · Label holders, mini eyelets (Making Memories) · Rhinestones · Foam adhesive · Wendy font (Adobe)

Brown: The humblest of colors, brown derives from the soil. Drawn from the very substance of our world, this unpretentious color can be described as nurturing, wholesome, hard-working and practical. It can range from the slightly bland and utilitarian side of beige to rich and hearty chocolate shades. Brown's steady comfort is associated with hearth and home.

White: Considered delicate and pristine, white shows itself in nature in the clouds and snow. White can symbolize innocence, cleanliness, purity and holiness. Because of these traits, both brides and medical personnel traditionally wear white.

Gray: Subtle and slightly mysterious, gray is associated with twilight, moonbeams and fog. Conjuring feelings ranging from drab to serene, gray is never gaudy, even in the form of silver. The coolest of the neutrals, gray is a subdued color that evokes quiet and introspection.

Black: Drawn from the dark of night, black can be both practical and dramatic. It raises a wide spectrum of feelings, since one person might see it as foreboding and solemn while another might see it as elegant and mysterious. Either way, black is undeniably powerful. A dynamic partner to the spectrum colors, black has deep and sophisticated overtones.

Drawn primarily from their existence in the natural world, each color has its own voice. The resulting emotional responses cross cultural boundaries and can be used effectively in design. Learn the feelings associated with color, and then use those messages to support your layout themes.

savvy color tricks

Consider these tips when designing with color:

✳ Because of its high intensity, yellow (like white) can act as a bright note to attract attention to a focal point.

✳ Too much blue in a design can feel sterile or melancholy, so add of dash of energy with warm color accents.

✳ A predominantly gray or brown color scheme can be effective to convey either subtle and introspective or earthy and wholesome moods, respectively, but on their own they might be bland. Spice them up with a variety of textures, shapes or colorful accents.

✳ Green can be used as both a prominent color or an almost neutral hue, just as we see it in nature.

✳ Neutrals can have slightly warm or cool overtones, so reinforce the overall color mood by choosing a neutral with a temperature that parallels the design's dominant color.

✳ If you are seeking dramatic impact, choose red for its attention-grabbing skills or purple for its lavish, mysterious nature.

✳ Too many colors in one design can send mixed messages and be disconcerting to the eye. For no-fail unity, keep color combinations to one main color with one or two accent colors. Or, mix two predominant colors with a neutral.

✳ An abundance of pure white can appear too stark and be hard on the eyes. Vary the temperatures of whites or add touches of a color or another neutral to soften it.

✳ Neutral colors can be added as accents in small doses to any color scheme without interfering with the fundamental color combination or meaning.

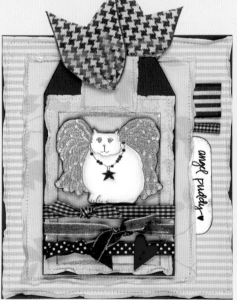

Jazz up a gray or other neutral-based palette with texture, patterns and touches of color, as illustrated on the left card. On the right card, neutral brown and ivory offer support but let the complementary red and green color scheme prominently come through.

Supplies: Gray, white, red, ivory cardstocks · Patterned papers: Liz King gray designs (EK Success), green paisley (Anna Griffin), red marble (Carolee's Creations), red gingham (Rusty Pickle) · Stamps (Paula Best) · Ultra-fine silver embossing powder (Stamp A Mania) · Angora watercolors (Canson) · Clear gloss medium (Ranger) · Ribbons · Woven tabs (Scrapworks) · Paper tab (Stampin' Up) · Button (Doodlebug Designs) · Heart punch (EK Success) · Postage decorative scissors (Fiskars) · Thread · Foam adhesive (3L) · Gray, brown, silver inks · Black, burgundy, brown markers

BRIDGING MANHOOD

Lori's thoughts about her 13-year-old son Steven:
It is fascinating to watch Steven become more a man everyday. His voice is becoming deeper, he grows taller by the week and he has muscles where baby fat used to be. His instant, bright smile, sparkling blue eyes and spattering of freckles make a handsome combination, which must be irresistible to any 13-year-old girl. Although he is certainly intelligent, he is more interested in socializing that actually getting his school work done. He rides his motorcycle as skillfully as a grown man and amazes everyone at his ability to master anything with wheels, even a unicycle. Best of all, Steven is a loving, thoughtful young man. When speaking to his great-grandparents his usually boisterous voice turns to a gentle tone that conveys how much he respects and cherishes them. He is always willing to help someone in need and looks out for the kids who are being picked on in school, sometimes at his own peril. He also looks out for his little sister, Sarah, and willingly plays with younger kids when the circumstance arises. Although he is now officially a teenager, he will still hug his mom in public, which I think is cool! May 2005

On this layout about my teenage nephew, texture and touches of red and green in the accents and photo keep the neutral palette from becoming boring. A color palette primarily consisting of brown hues echoes the pictured stonework and evokes a down-to-earth and wholesome mood. The layout's design and palette were inspired by the Mission-style architecture of the photograph's stone structure.

JOURNALING: LORI AUSTILL

Supplies: Dark brown cardstock (Prism Papers) · Light green, light brown, red cardstocks · Patterned papers: light brown (Vintage Workshop), dark brown (Stampin' Up!) · Thread · Foam adhesive (3L) · Ragged MF font · Parchment MF font · P22 Arts Ornaments Two font (P22 Type Foundry)

choose a color message

Since each color elicits its own emotional response, pick colors that will contribute to a layout's theme or mood.

red

exciting, passionate,
powerful, dramatic

orange

vibrant, energetic,
spirited, warm

yellow

outgoing, hopeful,
cheerful, glorious

white

pure, innocent,
silent, unsullied

gray

quiet, subdued,
reflective, peaceful

Supplies for all tags: Various colored cardstocks · Patterned papers · Paint chips · Stamps: cherries (A Stamp In The Hand), leaves (Kodomo), moon face (Hampton Art Stamps) · Butterfly die cut, teddy bear sticker (Paper House Productions) · Purple flower stickers (Autumn Leaves) · Silver filigree sticker (Mrs. Grossman's) · Jolee's yellow daisies (EK Success) · Micro beads · Laminate chips · Green acrylic tile (Junkitz) · Heart button (Doodlebug) · Acrylic buckles (KI Memories) · Metal roses, velvet leaves (Artchix Studio) · Bottle cap, lemon sticker (Design Originals) · Metal moulding (Making Memories) · Metal tag (Magic Scraps) · Metal rimmed tags · Staples · Orange beaded flowers (Marcel Schurman) · Crocheted snowflakes (Wimpole Street Creations) · Ribbon · Rickrack · Mesh (Magic Mesh) · Skeleton leaves · Black dye ink · StazOn black solvent ink (Tsukineko) · Purple acrylic paint · Clear gloss medium · Foam adhesive

750F-7 D
Deep Space

440D-6 D
Grassy Field

440D-7 D
Vineyard

610D-6 D
Enduring

610D-7 ?

240F-6 A
Sable Brown

240F-7 D
Root Beer

650?-7 D
Mystical Purple

black

formal, sophisticated,
strong, serious

brown

natural, wholesome,
understated,
nurturing

green

fresh, fertile,
harmonious,
balanced

blue

refreshing, serene,
spiritual, cool

purple

mysterious,
splendorous,
mystical, decadent

You are a constant whirlwind, my Anneliese, but there are those few moments when you stop for a few seconds of reflection or to take time to absorb and process the mysteries of your 22-month-old world. Grandma Pesce calls this your "input mode", and I revel in these brief flashes of the quieter side of my energetic little girl. Usually you just glow with your boundless energy, but during these scarce quiet moments your inner beauty shines with the unique luminescence that can only belong to a toddler. I get a chance to study your face during this oh-so-fleeting time when you are between baby and little girl, and my heart basks in the chance to be still for a moment in your company. Then it passes and we are back to running and jumping, laughing and squealing. But the memories of those moments will always linger in a special place in my heart.

Pause

The sugar-spun tints of pale pink, celery, lavender and baby blue in this pastel color palette point to the tender age of two-year-old Anna while bringing a soft, feminine quality to the design. The subtle colors reinforce the quiet moment captured in the photos and cited in the title and journaling.

PHOTOS AND JOURNALING: MICHELLE PESCE

Supplies: Light pink, lavender cardstocks · Patterned papers: pink floral (K & Company), lavendar, green, pink polka dot (Anna Griffin) · Transparency (Grafix) · Clear buttons (7 Gypsies) · Thread · Floss · Photo corners · Acrylic paint · Agincort font · Migraine Serif font

color palettes

Choose a color scheme that supports your layout's mood

Picture the classic image of an artist: a figure dressed in a beret and splattered smock, standing at an easel, with a paint brush in one hand and a paint palette in the other. In this context, a palette is an oval board with a hole in the middle on which a painter squeezes her paints. As the artist works on a painting, she dabs a brush in one of the spots of color on the palette and applies it to the canvas. While the pigments she is using are laid out on this palette tool, those same hues make up the painting's color scheme, which is also called its color palette.

No matter which media a design is created in or what colors are involved, each design has its own unique color palette. That color palette might consist of a simple two-color combination or it might be like confetti, made up of a plethora of hues. The colors could be complementary tones or be a monochromatic array containing ten different shades of green. A color palette is simply the set of colors used in a design.

As a scrapbook artist, you create a layout's color palette in a process similar to a painter. You choose a group of colored papers and products for the design and then "dip" into them as you work, choosing one color for the background, one for journaling, another for photo mats and so on. Also like a painting, the colors in your layout can make a huge visual impact on the design. Since color plays such a significant role in the success of a page, how do you select the best color palette for a layout?

To illustrate how different color palettes can create entirely different moods, the scrapbook pages throughout this chapter consist of the same design executed in four distinct color palettes. On each version, the title, journaling and composition are alike. The photos are the same, but have been printed in either black-and-white or sepia to better mesh with each color scheme. For dramatic variation, each version has been created in shades chosen from one of the four basic color palette groups: jewel-tones, pastels, brights and earth tones.

While there may be several color schemes that are appropriate for any one layout, different palettes can be chosen to highlight particular aspects of a design's mood and theme. More than any other element of design, color has the ability to convey emotions, elicit memories and incite visual associations. Tap into that power to support the layout's foremost message. While there may not be a right or wrong color scheme for a page, the best choice is one that most successfully enforces the theme and mood of the design.

A jewel-toned color palette of amethyst, emerald, carnelian orange and ruby emphasizes the mood of a timeless childhood moment. Through their depth and old-fashioned appeal, these rich, full-bodied colors play up the reflective nature of the journaling and Anna's pensive expressions.

PHOTOS AND JOURNALING:
MICHELLE PESCE

Supplies: Dark purple, dark red cardstocks · Patterned papers (Anna Griffin) · Transparency (Grafix) · Clear buttons (7 Gypsies) · Thread · Floss · Photo corners (Kolo) · Acrylic paint · Agincort font · Migraine Serif font

consider photo colors

To begin choosing a color palette, first look at your photographs. You might select the whole color scheme based on something in a photo, such as pumpkins in the background or the hues in your daughter's dance costume. When using color photographs, pick colors that both complement the pictures and support the page theme. If it's difficult to do both, consider converting the photos to black-and-white or sepia. This simple change can allow better control over the color palette while keeping the focus on the subject matter. For example, what if the photo's subjects are wearing brightly colored clothing, while your intended layout theme is contemplative in nature? Desaturating the photos gives you the ability to choose a color palette that coordinates with your message, thus resolving the conflict and allowing for a more unified design in every aspect of the layout.

color in the world around you

In addition to your photos, color palette inspiration may come from a variety of sources. Note color schemes in fashion, advertisements, home decorating magazines, art museums and other interesting places. Simple observation of the world around you provides a starting point for fresh color palettes. Then you can utilize basic color theory to fine tune your choices.

Observe how the same designs shown here can feel different depending on the color palette. What aspects of the layout's theme do particular palettes emphasize or minimize? Pick a favorite palette. Now think about why you chose it. Is it personal preference? Is it the way you interpret the layout theme and mood? Or is it a bit of both? When choosing a palette for your own designs, pick colors that will most effectively "paint" the mood of the layout's story.

You are a constant whirlwind, my Anneliese, but there are those few moments when you stop for a few seconds of reflection or to take time to absorb and process the mysteries of your 22-month-old world. Grandma Pesce calls this your "input mode", and I revel in these brief flashes of the quieter side of my energetic little girl. Usually you just glow with your boundless energy, but during these scarce quiet moments your inner beauty shines with the unique luminescence that can only belong to a toddler. I get a chance to study your face during this oh-so-fleeting time when you are between baby and little girl, and my heart basks in the chance to be still for a moment in your company. Then it passes and we are back to running and jumping, laughing and squealing. But the memories of those moments will always linger in a special place in my heart.

A subdued earth tone color palette of saffron, olive green, wheat, and rust creates a warm, muted mood. The natural tones draw attention to the mellow moment captured in the photos and the thoughtful sentiments expressed in the journaling.

PHOTOS AND JOURNALING: MICHELLE PESCE

Supplies: Taupe, rust cardstocks · Patterned papers (Anna Griffin) · Transparency (Grafix) · Clear buttons (7 Gypsies) · Thread · Floss · Photo corners (Kolo) · Acrylic paint · Agincort font · Migraine Serif font

color combination resources
Find color palettes from across the ages and around the world in these design books.

Color Index
by Jim Krause, HOW Design Books

Living Colors: The Definitive Guide to Color Palettes through the Ages
by Margaret Walch and Augustine Hope, Chronicle Books

The Designer's Guide to Color Combinations
by Leslie Cabarga, HOW Design Books

The Designer's Guide to Global Color Combinations
by Leslie Cabarga, HOW Design Books

The Scrapbooker's Essential Guide to Color
Memory Makers Books

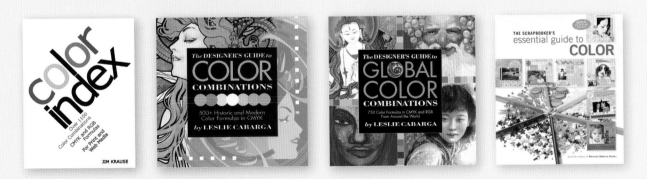

ou are a constant whirlwind, my Anneliese, but there are those few moments when you stop for a few seconds of reflection or to take time to absorb and process the mysteries of your 22-month-old world. Grandma Pesce calls this your "input mode", and I revel in these brief flashes of the quieter side of my energetic little girl. Usually you just glow with your boundless energy, but during these scarce quiet moments your inner beauty shines with the unique luminescence that can only belong to a toddler. I get a chance to study your face during this oh-so-fleeting time when you are between baby and little girl, and my heart basks in the chance to be still for a moment in your company. Then it passes and we are back to running and jumping, laughing and squealing. But the memories of those moments will always linger in a special place in my heart.

A bright color palette sparkles with the bold and vibrant playfulness of sunny yellow, lime, juicy orange and hot pink. This color scheme highlights the journaling's contrast between Anna's usual high energy and this moment of stillness.

PHOTOS AND JOURNALING: MICHELLE PESCE

Supplies: Bright pink, yellow, orange cardstocks · Patterned papers: yellow design (KI Memories), pink, green, multi-colored designs (Anna Griffin) · Transparency (Grafix) · Clear buttons (7 Gypsies) · Thread · Floss · Photo corners · Acrylic paint · Agincort font · Migraine Serif font

basic color palettes

Compare how similar designs on these tags can have different moods depending on the color palettes.
Use the color swatches from each group to inspire a color palette for your next layout.

Vibrant brights consist of concentrated, vivid colors in pure hues that are energetic, bold and intense.

Muted earth tones are mellow and organic shades from nature that create a classic, subdued appearance.

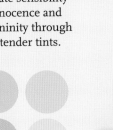

Subtle pastels offer a gentle, delicate sensibility of innocence and femininity through soft, tender tints.

Rich jewel-tones utilize full-bodied, saturated colors inspired by precious stones to convey depth and classic sophistication.

principles of design

4

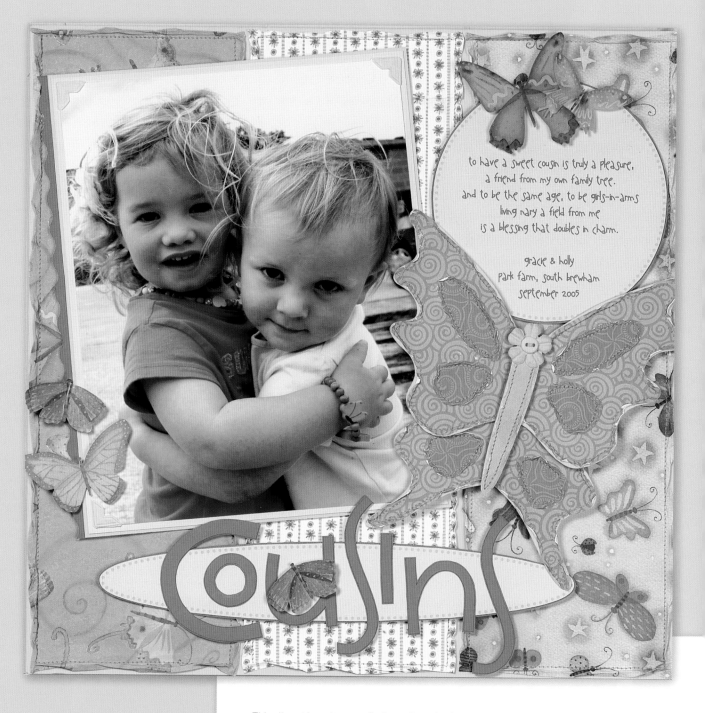

to have a sweet cousin is truly a pleasure.
a friend from my own family tree.
and to be the same age, to be girls-in-arms
living nary a field from me
is a blessing that doubles in charm.

gracie & holly
park farm, south brewham
september 2005

Cousins

This vibrant layout uses a fool-proof emphasis technique in which the focal point is placed in a "sweet spot." To find a sweet spot in a design, first mentally divide the space into vertical or horizontal thirds. The space where two of those thirds meet is visually appealing since it is neither too centered nor too close to the edge.

Supplies: Yellow, pink, orange cardstocks · Patterned papers: John Christopher butterfly prints (Paper Adventures), Jone Hallmark floral stripe (Creative Imaginations), orange swirl (Frances Meyer), pink design (Anna Griffin), turquoise and green dot (Treehouse Designs) · John Christopher butterfly stickers (Paper Adventures) · Photo corners (Kolo) · Paper flower (Prima) · Button · Wavy decorative scissors · Thread · Foam adhesive (3L) · Solea font · Rhino Dino font

emphasis & focal point

Show off the star of your layout

Imagine you are attending the ballet, such as a performance of Swan Lake. As the lights came up and the ballet begins, all eyes are drawn to the lithe form of the prima ballerina. Among a cast of graceful forms, the audience clearly perceives this beauty as the star. All aspects of the production point to her importance—the strongest spotlight is on her, her costume is more elaborate and bright, and the other dancers' movements diverge from her placement on the stage. Just as every theatrical production pivots around a main character, a successful scrapbook layout should have a strong focal point.

The focal point is the area on a layout that first catches the viewer's attention—it says "look at me!" That spot draws the eye into the design and causes the viewer to look further. The center of interest should express the most important aspect of the story the design is telling. The focal point makes an impact on the viewer and acts as the axis for the entire composition. Without a clear focus, a design can be boring or confusing. On scrapbook pages, the focal point is usually a photograph. Whether you are making a single photo layout or fitting in twelve shots, the same guidelines apply.

how to create focus

A focal point is created by contrast, which is the result of one element being different in some way from other elements of the design. Contrast can be created through four methods—size, color, line and shape, and placement. These methods can also be combined to create even greater impact. Take a look at how to use the different kinds of contrast within a scrapbook layout to make a successful focal point.

size

A straightforward approach to creating a focal point is simply to increase an element's size. The largest element of a composition is naturally dominant and thus is visually most important. On scrapbook pages, this is easily achieved by enlarging one photograph. On the "Wild Bunch" layout (page 94), the focal point is unmistakable even across a two-page spread because of one photo's prominent size.

color

The eye is first drawn to the lightest point of color or the place of highest contrast in a composition. By placing a light or bright color around your focal point, your focus is clearly emphasized. Adding a photo mat, corner accents or other embellishments that highlight the photo, such as a ribbon across the bottom edge, are simple ways to achieve this.

The light color will stand out even more when it is in high contrast to the other colors in the design. For example, a bright pink photo mat creates a stronger effect

With multiple photographs across a two-page spread, it is even more important to have a clear focal point. On this layout, emphasis is created by size, with the photo of the triplets together being the largest element in the spread.

PHOTOS: MICHELLE PESCE; JOURNALING: BARBARA CURRAN

Supplies: White cardstock · Green cardstocks (Prism Papers) · Ethan Kate patterned papers (Scrapworks) · Bamboo clips (Anima Designs) · Animal stamps (Stamps Happen) · Angora watercolors (Canson) · Nick Bantock Van Dyke brown ink (Ranger) · Green ribbon (Michaels) · Gingham ribbon (KI Memories) · Corner rounder (EK Success) · Foam adhesive (3L) · Thread · Charlie font · Socially Awkward font

when it is against dark gray or black patterned paper. High contrast can also work in the opposite manner. A dark color will stand out against a light one, as long as there is not a competing light or bright spot elsewhere in the design. An example would be to mat the central photo in black against a pale green background.

line and shape

An area that is different from the overall pattern of the design gets immediate attention. Vary the shape of the focus area to create such a distinction. You can achieve this by contrasting shapes or line quality. For example, place a vertical photo among predominantly horizontal lines, put a geometric form against organic or free-form shapes, or add a textured area on top of a smooth background. The "Think Pink" layout on page 97 uses an oversized circle shape to distinguish its focal point from the rectangles in the rest of the design.

placement

Where you choose to put the focal point in a design will influence its effectiveness. There are several different ways to use placement to create an area of emphasis, including direction, isolation and finding the "sweet spot."

Every composition has its own "sweet spot," which is the place where the focal point works best. Putting the focus right in the center can be a bit contrived and boring, but putting it too close to the edge can draw the eye right off the page. However, if you mentally divide your layout space into thirds, either horizontally or vertically, the sweet spot falls approximately in the middle of two of the adjoining thirds. This spot is just right: not too central and not too close to the edge. Because of its proportional position, such an area is visually appealing to the eye. The "Cousins" layout (page 92) utilizes this emphasis technique, placing the focal point photo at a jaunty angle centered between the first two vertical thirds of the page. See page 96 for a sweet spot diagram.

Another way to draw the eye to the focal point is by making supporting elements point to the main focus. This effect can be created very subtly, for example, by placing leaf accents pointing toward an image or, quite intentionally, like a radial composition in which the spokes of a wheel all converge together at the point of emphasis.

Isolation also creates a focal point because one element sits apart from the others. The element does not have to be different (it can be the same size, color and shape), but its placement draws attention. On the "Grandma's House" layout (below), all four photos are identical in size and execution, but the tilted photo automatically draws attention and becomes the focal point.

emphasis with unity

Even though contrast creates emphasis, remember that the focal point should also be an extension of the overall design. It is important to maintain unity in the design while setting the focal point apart. If the focal point is too different, it will feel like an unrelated object. But if the contrast is too subtle, the design will be static or the eye will be confused about where to look first.

By repeating some aspect of the focal point in small doses in other areas of the layout, you can create visual harmony while still letting the main element stand out. For example, if the focal-point photo has a bright red mat, echo that in red button accents elsewhere on the page.

Make your focal point the star of the layout by employing contrast through size, color, line, shape and placement, but design it to be a cohesive part of the overall composition. Like the prima ballerina, the focal point is the one element that brings the whole story together.

Although the four photos in this design are identical in size, the photo at the bottom right garners more attention because its angle sets it apart from the others. If an element stands out or is isolated from its counterparts, it creates an area of emphasis.

Supplies: Black cardstock · Red cardstock (Bazzill) · Patterned papers: florals (Junkitz), red crackle (Flair Designs) · Paper flowers, buttons (Making Memories) · Thread · Black dye ink · Foam adhesive (3L) · Niederwald font · Cafecoco font

fool-proof focal points

Use these ideas to help you design strong focal points on your layouts.

❋ Enlarge the main photo for maximum visual effect. Try a 5" x 7" (13cm x 18cm) or 6" x 9" (15cm x 23cm) photo, or be dramatic and use a full-page panoramic photo.

❋ Mat the photo with a color that is in high contrast to the page background color scheme.

❋ Isolate the main photo in an area away from the other photos.

❋ Orient the focal-point photo differently than the supporting photos. Tilt it if the rest are straight; make it horizontal among predominantly vertical photos, etc.

❋ Crop the main photo into a contrasting shape, such as an oval or circle, to play against the rectangular shape of the other photos.

❋ Mat one photo in a distinct manner. Multi-layered mats and special photo corners will contrast with simpler mat treatments used elsewhere in the design.

❋ Place the main photo where converging lines meet.

❋ Place light- or bright-colored details on or near the focal point. Lay a ribbon across the photo or put a shiny accent in its corner.

❋ Make the main photo black-and-white to distinguish it among color shots, or vice versa.

❋ When in doubt, use a close-up shot as the focal point. A close-up has more impact than photos with distant subjects.

❋ If you have overlapping elements on your layout, make sure your focal-point photo stays on top.

❋ Place the focal point in a "sweet spot" somewhere between the first and middle thirds of the layout, as shown in the diagram below.

Sweet Spot Diagram

With its distinctive shape, the round flamingo photo draws the viewer's attention among the rectangles, creating a focal point. The central flamingo photo is further emphasized by the white mat and over-lapping, high-contrast title treatment.

Supplies: Gray, pink, white cardstocks · Patterned papers: Over the Moon pink designs (EK Success), black and white print (Paper Company) · Transparency (Grafix) · Pink tags (American Tag Company) · Stamps: flamingo (Inkadinkado), flowers (Stamps by Judith), postmarks (Stampington & Company) · Angora watercolors (Canson) · Postalz faux floral postage (Art Accents) · Gray photo corners · Pink buttons · Ribbon · Black ink · Thread · Foam adhesive · QuigleyWiggly font · Fontdinerdotcom font

fix your focal point

Are there distractions stealing the limelight from your star photo? Here are some ideas to put it back at center stage.

* If your subject is facing off the page, have the photo reprinted with the negative flipped (or do a horizontal flip on your computer) so that the subject's eyes lead onto the layout instead of away from it.

* Enlarge the image to allow you to crop in tighter on the subject.

* Use image-editing software to simplify a distracting background.

* Convert the photo to black-and-white or sepia to decrease conflicting colors and backgrounds.

* Emphasize the subject in a black-and-white photo by tinting it, either traditionally or with image-editing software.

* Brighten, open up the mid-tones or increase contrast with image-editing software to correct the color of an image.

While the sculpture shown on this layout is itself a play on scale and proportion, including people in the photograph gives the viewer a sense of the sculpture's size. Utilize scale in photography to effectively show an object's size, which in turn contributes to a layout's story.

Supplies: Red cardstock (Bazzill) · Brown, cream cardstocks · Polka dot paper (Chatterbox) · Canvas label stickers (7 Gypsies) · Gingham ribbon (Offray) · Alphabet stamps (Hero Arts) · Brown dye ink (Stampin' Up!) · Thread · Foam adhesive (3L) · Colwell font · Berylium font

"Let proportion be found not only in numbers and measures, but also in sounds, weights, times, and positions, and whatever force there is."
–Leonardo da Vinci

proportion & scale

Create effective size relationships with these design principles

I am continually captivated by the sculpture in front of the Denver Public Library. "The Yearling" by Donald Lipski depicts a life-size Pinto pony standing on the seat of a two-story, bright red child's chair. The sculpture capitalizes on two closely-related elements of design that are concerned with size: proportion and scale. The scale of the giant chair captures one's attention while the disparity in proportion between the two objects charms the eye.

Proportion and scale are used in all kinds of design, including scrapbook design. But unlike sculptors, scrapbookers typically design on a flat surface within standard layout dimensions. Still, proportion and scale are design elements that can help balance a layout and create visual dynamics. When creating a layout, the proportion and scale of each page element should be considered. A rub-on title that looks great on a card might be dwarfed when placed on a full-size layout. Size is relative, and proportion and scale put size into context.

proportion and scale basics

Proportion refers to the size relationships between the parts within a whole. On a layout, proportion is the size relationship between each of the elements. It also refers to how those elements relate to the dimensions of the page. For example, proportion is at play when you consider whether or not the size of a page element overwhelms your photos.

Scale refers to the size of an element as it relates to units of measurement. For example, each of the cards shown on the next page utilize patterned paper with a daisy motif. On the center card, the daisy motif is of normal scale, meaning it is relative to the size of a normal daisy. On the left card, the motif is small scale; on the right card, it is large scale.

In scrapbooking, scale is apparent in the size of motifs, patterns or other common elements, such as tags or lettering. An artist may intentionally employ scale to create a dramatic effect or to result in a subtle rhythmic pattern. For example, the far right card below uses patterned paper with a larger-than-life daisy. The large-scale daisy, especially when used on a smaller format such as this card, is unusual and therefore eye-catching.

proportion in design

Effective use of proportion is the simplest way to balance a design and create a focal point. A large element in relation to other aspects of the design naturally garners the most attention. Use proportion by enlarging the focal-point photo or by creating the illusion of a larger photo via mats or frames. When using multiple photos, create this kind of natural hierarchy by planning for one large central photo along with smaller supporting images.

You can also use proportion to accentuate details in a design. In "Old Paint," on page 101, the hoof details of a broken china mosaic horse are emphasized in a large close-up photo of that area. If the photo sizes were switched, with the horse's head in the large photo and the hoof becoming a support image, the focus of the layout would shift accordingly.

When working with proportion, maintain balance between all of the elements. Let the focal point take the main stage and then size other elements to complement it. Those supporting elements should neither overwhelm the focal point nor be weak in comparison. In the disproportionate version of "Natural Charm," on page 102, the large flower accent draws more attention than the photo. This was corrected by increasing the size ratio between the photo and title in accordance to the size of the flower accent.

scale in design

In design, scale provides variety. If too many elements of a design are the same size, the eye is not compelled to move around the composition, and the design is boring.

Scale can be applied in a variety of ways to attract attention. Use small-scale elements to create delicate or intricate looks that entice the viewer with detail. Or repeat a small-scale motif to create a rhythmic pattern. Use large-scale elements to generate dramatic, eye-catching looks and images with an almost abstract sensibility. Compare the effect of the multiple small-scale details of "Grandma's Sweetheart" on page 103 to that of the singular grand statement of the stitched flower on "Natural Charm."

When composing and cropping photos, consider how scale might add emphasis and interest to the subject. For example, put the size of a baby's feet into context by comparing them to the size of her mother's hands. The Scale Contrast photo on page 102 is a charming example. Scale comparison can also be seen on "The Yearling" (page 98). The people standing under the giant chair provide an instant point of reference to the sculpture's height.

Keeping these elements of design in mind, evaluate your compositions to decide if the individual parts work together successfully. Whether your design has intricate details or dramatic large-scale motifs, keep everything in perspective with scale and proportion.

compare scale effects

Each of these cards uses patterned paper featuring daisies, but each pattern is in a different scale. The small-scale daisies on the first card create a low-key pattern. The large-scale daisy on the last card creates a nearly abstract design, while the middle card shows daisies in a realistic size. Though the cards feature the same motif and colors, they look distinctly different due to the varying scales.

| small scale | normal scale | large scale |

Supplies: Orange cardstock · Patterned papers: small daisy (NRN Designs), medium daisy (Kangaroo & Joey), large daisy (Hambly Studios) · Ribbon · Thread

teacup handle heels

Among the more than thirty fine steeds that were part of the "A Horse, Of Course" project in Billings, Montana over the summer of 2002, Old Paint was my favorite. Old Paint is covered in a mosaic of broken china pieces, created by local artist Maureen Baker. I particularly like the clever ways in which the artist incorporated the forms of some pieces of china into the shape of the horse, with the teacup handle heels and facial markings being striking examples. After standing in prominent spots around town for three months, the horses were sold at auction as a fundraiser to benefit the restoration of the historic Billings Depot.

Old Paint

This layout uses proportion to emphasize the page subject. Since the page focuses on the whimsical details of the horse sculpture, the close-up photo of the hoof was enlarged, thereby causing those special touches to take center stage. Smaller accent photos show the entire horse and put the close-up in perspective.

Supplies: Blue, white cardstocks · Patterned paper scraps · Gray dye ink (Stampin' Up!) · Thread · Button · Ribbon · Foam adhesive · Brubeck AH font

convey scale in your photographs

How small is your newborn baby or how big is that prize pumpkin? Whether you are taking posed photos or spontaneous snapshots, look for opportunities to show scale, since size is most effectively conveyed in relative terms. Michelle Pesce, photographer and 2004 Memory Makers Master, offers the following tips and examples for capturing scale in your photos:

* To show dramatic differences in scale, utilize people or commonplace objects as a reference point when shooting grand scenes like landscapes or architecture.

* Create the effect of scale contrast by shooting two objects that are similar but different in size. Place the objects side-by-side and then get on the same level as the subjects to take the picture.

* For realistic scale comparison between a person and an object, place the person at a similar distance from the camera as the object. Otherwise, if the person is close to the camera while the object is far away, the two will appear similar in size.

* Show off the gradation in size of a series of people or objects by lining them up from smallest to largest.

| point of reference | scale contrast | graduation of size |

proportion comparison

Compare the dynamics in the two versions of this layout. The oversized quilted flower grabs attention, but its scale demands that the proportions of the other elements also be strong to create a balanced composition. On the left version, the flower overpowers the photo and the title feels weak. On the right, the photo was enlarged to become the clear focal point and the title was given a bolder stature.

PHOTO: KELLI NOTO

Supplies: Gold cardstock · Patterned papers (Basic Grey) · Quilt batting · Thread · Brown dye ink · Foam adhesive · Airfoil Script SSK font

Grandma's SWEETHEART

My dear little Zoe, as sweet as can be
Her big violet eyes have their own special hue
They sparkle with joy as she peers up at you
She wrinkles her nose and giggles with glee
She babbles and babbles incessantly
I haven't a clue what she is saying
But she never stops talking, even while playing
She's constantly moving, always in action
Stopping only to check my reactions
Always so happy and full of great cheer
Somewhere in those words I can't quite hear
I know is 'Grandma, I love you!'
And I love you, too.

The small-scale details of the chocolates in crumpled wrappers, buttons and strips of hand-written translations of "sweet" all draw the viewer in for a closer look. Grouping these small elements into a border creates a rhythmic single unit that is proportional to the large photo and journaling block.

PHOTO: KELLI NOTO; JOURNALING POEM: SHARI POLLARD

Supplies: Brown, pink, white, ivory cardstocks · Patterned papers (Anna Griffin) · Chocolates, candy wrapper stamps (Rubber Baby Buggy Bumpers) · Stamp 'N Stuff brown embossing powder (Mark Enterprises) · Ultra fine clear embossing powder (Stamp A Mania) · Brown, platinum pigment ink · Angora watercolors (Canson) · Walnut ink · Colored pencils · Mini eyelets, buttons (Making Memories) · Ribbon · Thread · Paper crimper · Photo corners · Foam adhesive (3L) · Reynold Art Deco font · Speedball No 3 font

the best

meet my lovely parents, connie and tracy hansen. they have shown me integrity and faith, courage and humor. they have taught how important relationships are through their example. married over forty years and they consider each other to be their best friend. they are so beautiful to me, such an inspiration. i am blessed to have the best.

photo shoot with kelli noto september, 2004

In the background of this page, strips of light green and dark rust paper create an alternating rhythm. Strong vertical line quality exists where the paper strips meet and are stitched together, producing additional rhythm. The mica and fabric-ribbon embellishments on the photo mats create textural points of a visual triangle to direct the eye around the three photographs.

PHOTOS: KELLI NOTO

Supplies: Rust, sage cardstocks · Patterned papers: rust diamond (K & Company), sage floral (Colors by Design) · Mica shapes (USArtQuest) · Transparency (Grafix) · Fabric · Rust thread · Sage acrylic paint · Foam adhesive · Really Rust dye ink pad (Stampin' Up!) · Pretty Baby font

rhythm

Make your layouts dance with repeated elements

Last summer I got hooked on a television show called "So You Think You Can Dance." Each week the contestants, from a wide range of dance backgrounds and specialties, had to learn a new dance style and routine. It was great fun to see one person do street-wise hip-hop choreography while the next performed an old-fashioned Viennese waltz. Though the dance styles and the accompanying music were vastly different, they all had infectious rhythm in common. Whether dancing disco or a fox trot, rhythm provides a repeating tempo and unified structure that keeps the dancer moving with the song.

Rhythm is also a principle of design. But in design, rhythm causes your eye—not your body—to move. Simply stated, rhythm creates eye movement through the repetition of elements in a design. Incorporate rhythm into your page design to create patterns for the eye to follow. If used effectively, design rhythm will unify a layout via repeating elements, just like musical rhythm creates a structure to guide a melody.

Those repeated elements in a design might be page accents. They also could be executed through elements such as color, shape, texture or line. This repetition will help unify a design by lending cohesiveness to all of its singular elements.

characteristics of rhythm

Rhythm in design comes in three varieties: simple, progressive and alternating. All three types of rhythm are based on repetition. It is the way in which the elements recur that is specific to each type. Each method of applying rhythm can be used on its own, or combined for greater impact.

Simple rhythm consists of basic repetition, such as the chartreuse shutters on "Hemingway House" (page 107). These paper accents create a straightforward sense of rhythm because they duplicate each other.

Progressive rhythm creates a sequential pattern, meaning a recurring element changes in a regular manner. For instance, a color that moves from light to dark or a shape that progressively becomes larger are good examples of progressive rhythm. In "Views of the Dance Floor" on page 106, the central horizontal border moves the eye progressively across the layout as the flowers decrease in size from left to right.

Create alternating rhythm by rotating two elements in regular intervals. This will result in an even sequence. Achieve this rhythm by alternating smooth and rough textures, low and high color values, organic and geometric shapes, or light and dark colors. An alternating rhythmic background was created on "The Best" (page 104), by alternating light and dark colors of patterned papers in vertical strips. The checkered fabric ribbons also alternate in the same colors to echo this effect.

While rhythm contributes to the continuity of a design, remember to spice it up with a little variety within the repeated elements. The embellished squiggly metal pieces

On this page from my wedding album, the repetition of colors, patterns and textures—the flowers, ribbons and metal—creates rhythm and unity in the design. Progressive rhythm is shown in the flower border through increases in size, guiding the eye along the line of flowers.

Supplies: Green cardstock · Patterned papers: polka dot, trellis (Kangaroo & Joey), Jone Hallmark small floral print (Creative Imaginations), plaid (Karen Foster Design) · Vellum, transparency (Grafix) · Eco Africa metal accents (Provo Craft) · Paper flowers (Savvy Stamps) · Flower punches (EK Success, Emagination Crafts, Family Treasures) · Gingham ribbons (May Arts) · Green polka dot ribbon · Pearl buttons · White, clear thread · Green pen · Foam adhesive · CAC Shishoni Brush font

on "Views of the Dance Floor" (above) are similar overall, but they differ slightly due to the varying placement of the ribbons and flowers. These variations make the accents visually interesting and draw the eye.

rhythm & the elements of design

Since the elements of design are the building blocks for any visual composition, color, shape, line and texture can be used as vehicles to create rhythm.

Color: Pick a color that coordinates or contrasts with the dominant color on the page to use as a spot color in several areas such as photo mats or corners, smaller page accents or as a title background. Light or bright colors will immediately draw the eye to the pattern made by the color accents.

Shape: This element can be used in several ways to produce a rhythmic design. Because recurring elements do not always have to be identical to be effective, shape can be incorporated into various aspects of a design. For example, the layout might use circular shapes in several ways, such as on its patterned paper's print, the look of the typeface and the form of its embellishments. The shape of your photos also can serve as recurring shapes.

Line: Create rhythm through both line quality and direction. For line quality, stick with a consistent kind of edge for subtle repetition. You might use soft, torn edges in one layout or straight, clean edges in another. Repeat line direction as another means to produce rhythm. Looking again at "Views of the Dance Floor," you can see that both line direction and line quality are used. The page has repeated horizontal lines and straight, simple edges. Compare those clean edges to the softer stitched, vertical lines in the background of "The Best" (page 104).

Texture: Whether it is an embossed paper, a fuzzy fiber or shiny metal tags, texture can be recruited for the sake of rhythm when those tactile elements are repeated on a layout. The three-dimensional paper shutters on "Hemingway House" act as visual beats that move the eye through the spread.

Even if you personally don't have rhythm, your pages can if you follow these guidelines. Employing a single, strong group of repeated elements will yield dynamic results. Or team up several strong groups for even greater continuity. By designing with rhythm, your layouts will have a resounding tempo, resulting in flowing eye movement and a unified structure.

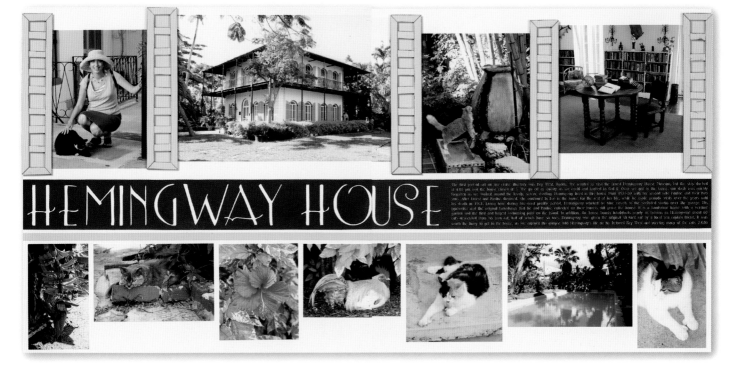

Repetition of texture and a spot color provides rhythm across this two-page layout. The dimensional chartreuse green shutter accents create a tempo of visual beats, effectively moving the eye across the spread. The paper shutters were created to mimic those of the historic house featured on the layout.

Supplies: White, chartreuse cardstocks (Prism Papers) · Mellow Moss dye ink (Stampin' Up!) · Foam adhesive (3L) · Lemon Chicken font · Florentine font

tips for no-fail rhythm

❋ **use it once, use it again**
If you use an element once, repeat it somewhere else. For example, if you use gingham ribbon as a tag top in one area, tie it through a button elsewhere in the layout. The eye will automatically connect related objects.

❋ **connect the dots**
Place recurring elements so that they create a visual shape, such as a triangle or quadrangle.

The eye will travel the implied path of these shapes, establishing circuitous movement throughout the design.

❋ **odd but true**
Repeat similar elements in odd-numbered amounts rather than even, since the eye finds this math more appealing. Groups of three are especially effective.

create rhythm on your layouts

These tags summarize ways to incorporate rhythm into a design.

Alternate patterns or light and dark colors. Bands of black and gold alternate.

Create a color, value or size progression, like the descending value of flowers.

Create a visual triangle. Visually connect the three stamped images and a triangle will form.

Repeat similar textures, such as bamboo paper and gold metal.

Supplies for all tags: Black, red, jade cardstocks · Gold printed cardstock (Hambly Studios) · Printed mulberry paper · Japanese papers (Moote Points) · Bamboo paper (Be Unique)· Polka dot paper (Colorbök) · Stamps: large oriental character (Stampabilities), goldfish (Rubberstamp Ave.), three geishas, medium oriental characters (Stampin' Up!), water bird (Picture Show), lantern (Rubber Stampede), all square images (Paula Best) · Chinese coin · Gold tag (Stampin' Up!) · Ultra-fine black embossing powder (Ranger) · Black dye, pigment inks · Colored pencils · Angora watercolors (Canson) · Ribbons · Jacquard ribbon (Wrights) · Flower punch (Marvy) · Gold eyelets and brads · Foam adhesive (3L)

Repeat line direction and/or quality with repetitive vertical lines.

Duplicate a motif, such as oriental characters, in multiple places.

Duplicate touches of spot color, as illustrated by teal highlights.

Echo similar shapes throughout a design. Circular shapes unite the patterns.

Clutch of Four

day four

about to fly the coup

day 14

Turdus Migratorius

2004 Robin Report

Radial balance is a natural fit for this layout about new life in a bird's nest. The images radiating out from the photo in the top right corner show the development of the baby birds in steps. The curve of the paper nest further emphasizes the circular shapes and gives the page design structure.

Supplies: Teal, brown cardstocks · Lotta Jansdotter labels, stationery set (Chronicle Books) · Oval paper clips (Making Memories) · Le Plume brown, teal pens (Marvy) · Foam adhesive · Paper crimper

balance

Create layouts with symmetry and equilibrium

have you ever watched a television program about Australia and marveled at the odd yet effortless bearings of the kangaroo? This creature must be one of the strangest looking animals on earth, and yet it bounds through the outback with speed and agility. The kangaroo is a working example of how balance can affect design. Its large, muscular tail acts to asymmetrically balance its forward motion and long feet.

But the kangaroo isn't the only example of successful balance in nature. Think of a daisy's perfect ring of petals that creates radial balance, or tree bark with its nubby texture of all-over symmetry. The many examples of balance in the natural world all testify to its importance in unity and its impact on design. As a scrapbooker, you are designing layouts rather than marsupials, but balance is just as important to the success of your pages.

A significant component of any successful composition is balance, with that balance contributing to the unity of the overall design. Our eye is naturally pleased by balance, and when it is absent, we feel a sense of dissatisfaction.

Balance is achieved when a design has an equal distribution of visual weight throughout its composition. In a scrapbook layout, the best way to see how the distribution falls is to mentally divide the layout in half. You can do this whether the layout is a single page or a spread. Squint at the layout to help you see if it looks balanced on each side of the central axis. If successful, the two sides will have a sense of equilibrium. First try this method with a vertical center line, then with a horizontal one. Be aware that because of our sense of gravity, our eye often prefers the bottom half to be a little heavier than the top.

Divide the design in half, and it works like an old-fashioned scale, with each side having the power to tip it one way or the other depending on what the elements "weigh." The different elements in the design each have their own visual weight. The corresponding elements do not have to be exactly alike to be equal, but rather have similar visual impact depending on how they are used, or what they visually weigh. Items weigh more or less depending on factors such as their color, value, size, shape, texture and placement. For example, white is lighter than black and a thickly striped print is heavier than a petite-dot pattern.

There are several approaches to distributing elements and visual weight in a design in order to achieve equilibrium. The three types of balance are symmetrical, asymmetrical and radial. Let's define each type and look at how it works to bring balance to a layout.

symmetrical

Symmetrical balance is like a mirror image, with the shapes and their positions on either side of the central axis being the same. The elements on each side can vary slightly without changing the symmetry. The focal point is emphasized within this even composition by its position on the central axis.

There are two types of symmetrical balance: bilateral and crystallographic (that's the big word for today!). Bilateral balance is truly a mirror image, like the human body, with each side reflecting the other. Crystallographic balance consists of an all-over pattern. Like the texture of tree bark, visual weight and value patterns are evenly distributed throughout the design. The layout "Grandma & Grandpa Chris" (below) uses crystallographic balance to organize a series of detailed tags into a cohesive design. Each tag varies slightly, but the overall value structure is the same throughout the layout, creating the all-over pattern indicative of this kind of symmetrical balance.

Symmetrical balance is sometimes referred to as formal balance due to its sense of dignified, quiet simplicity. It is the easiest type of balance to execute and can be a solution when you need to organize complex or busy elements into a unified composition. While its repetition can bring structure, it can also lack variety, sometimes resulting in a static and contrived appearance. Symmetrical balance, in both bilateral and crystallographic versions, offers a straightforward approach to visual equilibrium in a design.

asymmetrical

Asymmetrical balance is more complex, requiring the artist to balance dissimilar objects on each side of a central axis. To illustrate this type of balance, think again of our funny kangaroo, an angular flamingo, or the sweep of a coral reef. The informal nature of asymmetrical balance makes it appear more natural and spontaneous than symmetrical balance, but it involves more consideration to achieve. In order to affect the weight on each side of an asymmetrical layout, several techniques can be employed, usually together in some combination: color, shape, position, texture, value and typography.

By color: Small areas of dark or dull color can balance a large area of light or bright color. Color is especially useful, allowing for a great difference in shapes that still are balanced due to the color applied to each of them.

In order to include multiple photos on this layout about my grandparents, I utilized a series of tags. Even though the tags are not identical, they are organized in a unified way, employing crystallographic balance. The variety among the tags prevents the symmetrical structure from looking static.

Supplies: Red, teal cardstocks · Patterned papers: black design (Frances Meyer), teal floral (Anna Griffin) · Epoxy letter stickers (K & Company) · Metal corners (Magic Scraps, Making Memories) · Photo turns (7 Gypsies) · Metal stencil letter C (Colorbök) · Key (Li'l Davis Designs) · Gingham covered buttons (MOD) · Heart eyelet charm (Making Memories) · Ribbons (May Arts, Offray, Renaissance Ribbons, vintage) · Printed ribbon (Boxer Scrapbook Productions) · Rose stamp (Club Scrap) · Square hole punch (Fiskars) · Black ink · Black pen · Foam adhesive · Georgia font

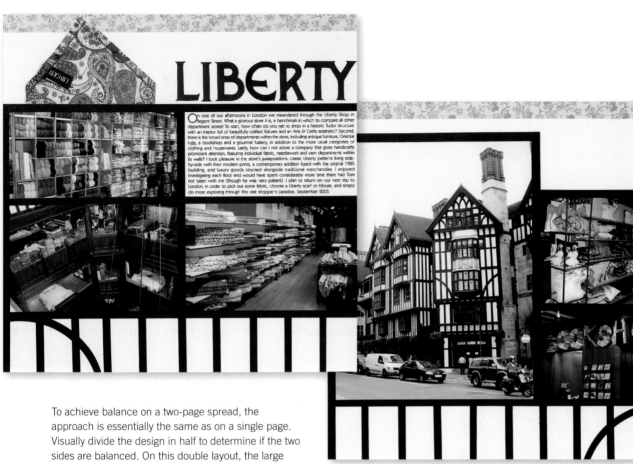

To achieve balance on a two-page spread, the approach is essentially the same as on a single page. Visually divide the design in half to determine if the two sides are balanced. On this double layout, the large photo and title/journaling area balance each other in this nearly symmetrical composition.

Supplies: White, black cardstocks (Prism Papers) · Floral paper (Anna Griffin) · Thread · Kabel Book font · Handkerchief

By shape: Smaller, more intricate shapes have more visual weight than larger, simpler shapes. Since the eye is drawn to the shape with more detail, a 3" (8cm) kidney shape results in more visual impact than a 10" (25cm) circle.

By position: Time to apply some physics. A large item placed closer to the center can be balanced by a smaller item placed near the edge. Balance by position appears especially uncontrived.

By value and texture: An object with high contrast is more eye-catching, and thus visually heavier, than an item that has low contrast. In the same manner, an element with dark and light variations is more visually interesting than a smooth, unrelieved surface, such as a red patterned paper versus a plain red cardstock.

By typography: The text of a title or journaling block creates visual texture, with its type style and density influencing its visual weight. Try viewing these typography elements with squinted eyes in order to see beyond their words and determine their visual weight.

radial

Radial balance is abundant in nature, bringing to mind starfish, snowflakes and all kinds of flowers. In radial balance, the elements circle out from a central focal point. Depending on the focus, radial balance can be either symmetrical or asymmetrical. See "The Robin Report" (page 110) for an example of asymmetrical radial balance. This type of balance works well to create an organized composition that also expresses energy, but should be used in an understated manner in order to avoid an obvious feel.

In order to create a pleasing, well-proportioned scrapbook layout, balance is a key principle in its design. Whether symmetrical, asymmetrical or radial in nature, balance brings equilibrium to the composition and contributes to the unity of the page. With practice, you may balance your layouts as swiftly as a kangaroo hops.

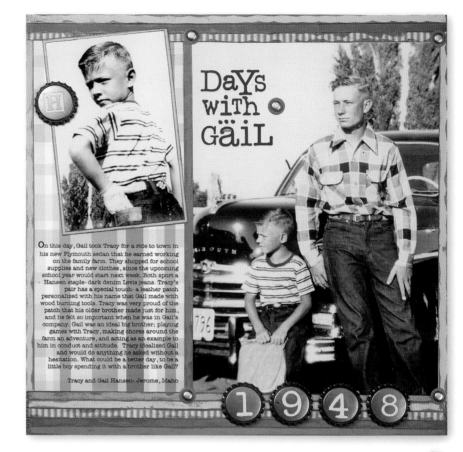

This layout is asymmetrically balanced through the use of value and pattern. If visually divided down the center, it can be seen that the light areas and patterns on the left side work to balance the dark forms in the lower part of the right-hand photo. The value patterns progress from light at the top of the page to darker tones at the bottom, with the paper strip and bottle cap border grounding the design.

Supplies: Patterned, solid papers (Chatterbox) · Copper ink (Tsukineko) · Copper embossing powder (Stamp A Mania) · Copper leafing pen (Krylon) · Rub-on letters (Autumn Leaves) · Green rivets (Chatterbox) · Transparency (Grafix) · Copper brads · Bottle caps · Foam adhesive · Dateline font

methods of balance

Various kinds of balance are shown on this set of feline tags.

Supplies: Rust, Kraft brown, black cardstocks · Patterned papers: green check, chartreuse floral (K & Co.), vintage label print (Deluxe Designs) · Cat postage, lion stamps (Paula Best) · Postage decorative scissors (Fiskars) · Angora watercolors (Canson) · Gingham fabric · Buttons · Fiber · Thread · Black ink · Foam adhesive

symmetrical bilateral

symmetrical crystallographic (all-over pattern)

asymmetrical by color

evaluate visual weight

Visual weight is like the saying "What weighs more: a pound of lead or a pound of feathers?" If the sizes of two elements are similar, it's the character of each item that affects its visual weight.

more visual weight

* dark or muted color
* textured surface
* intricate shape
* small element placed away from central axis
* area of high value contrast
* shiny surface

less visual weight

* light or bright color
* smooth surface
* simple shape
* large element near central axis
* area of low value contrast
* matte or dull surface

set the mood

Choose the method of balance for your composition based on the mood you want the layout to convey. To help you match up the appropriate method with a mood, here are descriptive words for each category.

symmetrical

* formal
* orderly
* serene
* dignified
* sedate
* solemn
* imposing
* austere

asymmetrical

* casual
* spontaneous
* dynamic
* natural
* having variety
* playful
* subtle
* uncontrived

asymmetrical by value and texture

asymmetrical by shape

asymmetrical by position

radial

For Jennifer, for the gypsy that you are, here are some lace
and paper flowers. A tribute to your bohemian heart, that side of you amongst the paradox
of a complex old soul. That part of you that is adorned in red, velvet and beads; that speaks with words like
Keats crossed with Kerouac; that sings and sways like Stevie. Together, my dearest friend, we can sail through the
changing ocean's tide and we'll handle the seasons of our lives. May you always knock on my window at midnight,
may we always commune over caffeine and nicotine, may we buy and steal many more shoes, and may
my crystalline knowledge of you only grow for another fourteen years and beyond.
To the gypsy that remains * Who faces freedom, with a little fear
I have no fear, I have only love

Although this layout contains many detailed aspects, the parts come together to create a unified design. The jewel-toned color scheme, intricate typography, rich textures and unique photo tinting work in tandem to create an elegant Bohemian sensibility. The unified sum of the layout's parts work together to create a mood and environment.

PHOTO: JENNIFER BOOTHE HATCH

Supplies: Dark red, teal, brown cardstocks · Patterned papers: teal floral (K & Company), red floral (Daisy D's) · Rose building stamp (Stamp A Mania) · Deckle edge scissors (Fiskars) · Red photo corners · Ribbon (Offray) · Tapestry fabric (Maruca Designs) · Red thread · Ultra-fine point black pen (Staedtler) · Foam adhesive · Brubeck AH font · Vein font

unity

Combine the elements and principles in harmony

In the midst of wedding plans, I worked with my florist to conceptualize the perfect bridal bouquet to complement my dress and the mood of the celebration. While the bouquet would have a mixture of different kinds of flowers, it would also be an arrangement unified by common factors and the overall design. The diversity in textures and shapes of flowers such as orchids, tulips, roses and Bells of Ireland provided variety within a monochromatic color scheme of spring green (yes, I had green flowers!). Each stem was an integral piece in the composition of the bouquet. Whether arranging flowers or crafting scrapbook layouts, the essence of creating harmony in a design is in finding unity.

Unity is the overseeing force of all the design elements and principles, governing how well they work together. Used in tandem with variety, unity brings the parts of your design together in perfect accord. Unity is the visual connection between the parts of a layout design, causing them to look like they belong together. It is harmony, wholeness and the heart of the composition.

When we view a design, our eye sees the piece as a whole before it takes in its parts. When doing so, our eye wants to find organization and unity. It does not like to see chaos. In designing scrapbook pages, your goal should be to make it natural for the eye to see the layout as an integrated whole. This is achieved by how well you organize the individual parts. Without unity, your layout is simply a collection of unrelated fragments.

While unity provides the framework for the design to flow together, too much unity on its own can be boring. Variety provides visual interest within unity's structure. Unity and variety depend on each other to create a balanced composition—not too static, not too chaotic. When designing a scrapbook layout, the distribution of unity and variety is flexible, and can produce different results in the mood of the page depending on where the emphasis lies. When planning a layout with a serene mood, more unity would make sense. But for a page depicting your family's visit to an amusement park, more variety is needed to express the energy of the day. Like two sides of the same coin, unity and variety are two facets in the process of creating a cohesive yet compelling design.

achieving unity

Proximity: The simplest route to creating unity in a design is to use proximity. By placing elements close to one another, you create a unit that the eye sees as a related pattern. Floating elements can be distracting from the overall design, but by employing proximity, you can ground those elements to each other. This is why borders are so effective for organizing a variety of page elements. For instance, look at "Sweet Feet," on page 119. If the different tags were randomly placed around the page, they might seem unrelated to each other and floating in space. By grouping them into a vertical border, they create one cohesive visual statement.

Repetition: Repetition is created by simply repeating an aspect of the design multiple times throughout the layout. The repeated elements should share the same fundamental characteristics, but do not have to be identical. For example, a layout could carry out a playful mood with recurring primary colors and spherical shapes. Red highlights could repeat in the photo mats and title, while a circular motif is seen in polka dot background paper, eyelets, round tags and a cropped round photo. Repeated elements should contribute to the theme of the design while creating visual continuity.

Continuation: A continuing line or form can also provide unity in a design. Whether the continuation is in an organic curve, a straight line, or a diagonal slash, it will carry the eye through the layout smoothly. One subtle example of this can be seen in print media, where graphic designers connect text blocks, photographs and illustrations by keeping the edges of all the objects aligned. Take a look at the book page you are reading to see this method in practice. This publishing trick can be easily adapted to your scrapbook layouts when you are planning the placement of its elements.

achieving variety

Contrast: Dramatic variety can be achieved by contrasting the elements of a design against each other. Classic contrast effects can be created by using different colors or value effects. Other means of contrasting elements in a layout are to juxtapose varying textures, fonts or patterns. The look of a floral pattern placed with a smooth stripe in a similar color family can be a dynamic combination. Think also of the tactile quality of a smooth metal tag against thick, embossed paper.

Variation: Visual interest can be created in conjunction with repetition by playing on a theme. Multiple variations of the same motif can have common traits, but for variety don't duplicate them exactly. For instance, daisy embellishments on a layout could be used in a small scale on the background paper and then again in a medley of page

This layout's design is unified through repetition and proximity. A snowflake motif repeats throughout the page, seen in both the title treatment and the hand-cut accents. Slight overlapping connects the photo, title and journaling. For variety, the distinctive teal lettering brings variation to the color scheme, while the large white snowflakes provide interesting contrast and negative shapes against the background paper.

PHOTO: DIGITAL VISION/GETTY IMAGES

Supplies: Burnt orange, dark teal, ivory cardstocks (Prism Papers) · Wild Asparagus patterned papers (My Mind's Eye) · Snowflake clip art (www.clipart.com) · Nick Bantock Van Dyke brown ink (Ranger) · Thread · Foam adhesive · Ballpark Weiner font · Architect font

An adventure in the city
A chilly day, about to snow
Whatever the weather
No matter where we might go
We always enjoy time together

Sweet Feet

You have tiny shoes with ribbons and bows and sweet little socks with patterns and lace, but I think I like your feet best of all when they are bare. With those soft, smooth heels and straight rows of tiny toes, it seems a shame to cover what God made so perfect. I always smile when I see them curling, flexing and kicking, as if your tiny feet are trying to communicate what you can't yet say. You just can't beat bare baby feet! May 2005

Stella

Six weeks old

accents ranging in size and materials. Subtle variations can be seen in a page that employs organic lines through a script font, torn paper edges, and a skeleton leaf accent.

As you've learned, unity, in conjunction with variety, can be achieved on any layout through several different methods. But unity also serves a broader purpose of providing structure to all other design elements and principles. That's why I've included it as the last chapter in this book. As you become more skilled in working with all aspects of design, you'll develop a stronger sense of what is needed to unify a page. When you can do that, your layouts will bloom with visual harmony every time.

Twill tape creates a vertical axis around which the asymmetrical composition unfolds. A charming mother-baby photo and a swirling script title sit on the left side. On the right, three different tags are assembled into a border unit. Each aspect of the design, from the line quality to the notes of rhythm, contributes to its harmonious mood and appearance.

PHOTOS: MICHELLE PESCE, JOURNALING: LYDIA RUEGER

Supplies: Black, teal cardstock · Patterned papers: teal polka dot (K & Company), black floral (Anna Griffin), black script (Rusty Pickle) · Vellum (Grafix) · Buttonhole, measuring tape twills (Carolee's Creations) · Ribbon · Kraft tag (Artifacts) · Photo corners · Ultra-fine point black pen (Staedtler) · Black dye ink · Thread · Foam adhesive · Constanza font

When designing two-page layouts, it is important to create unity across both halves. The two sides should feel that they belong together and the eye should travel throughout the entire piece. This spread is unified through repetition, which is found in its color scheme, textures, motifs and accents. In addition, the continuation of the bargello paper-pieced border across the bottom unites the two pages.

PHOTOS: JENNIFER BOOTHE HATCH

Supplies: Black, red cardstocks (Club Scrap) · Japanese papers (Moote Points) · Paper slide mounts (Design Originals) · Double stick adhesive sheet, vellum (Grafix) · Black jacquard ribbon, appliqués (Wrights) · Small charms (Artchix Studio) · Flat metal charms (American Traditional Designs) · Chinese character stamps (Stampabilities) · Gingham ribbon · Chopsticks · Black dye ink · Black pen · Clear gloss medium (Ranger) · Foam adhesive (3L) · Dauphin font · Bargello paper piecing technique on border from *Paper Delight*, by Cherryl Moote (Moote Points)

five methods for unity with variety

Unity brings the elements of a layout together, while variety adds some spice!

for unity: proximity
place elements close together or slightly touching so they feel like they belong together, or group individual pieces into units such as tags and borders

repetition
repeat similar elements, like color, texture, shape or line quality, throughout a composition

continuation
create flowing eye motion and tie a design together by carrying a line or form through a layout

for variety: contrast
play up a bit of difference, such as a dash of black in a monochromatic color scheme or one photo placed at a jaunty angle when the rest are in a perfect row

variation
use variation of a theme to repeat a design's motifs. For example, use a bevy of butterfly accents, but with each in a unique color.

relieve boredom and confusion

Identify and rectify common mistakes that contribute to inharmonious scrapbook layouts.

sticker sneeze

visual confusion caused by a scatter of stickers or other small accents placed randomly around a page

solution

Use proximity to corral stickers together in clusters, as a border or on tags.

odd man out

a layout that contains an element that just doesn't fit, causing disharmony and visual distraction

solution

Check that each component of the layout evokes descriptive adjectives that meld with the overall layout and mood. Replace the oddball element with a more appropriate choice.

lost in space

floating elements that seem to be unconnected and hanging in the space of the layout

solution

Anchor elements to each other, the photos, or other areas by overlapping or touching their edges. Visually ground them by fastening them to the page with eyelets, stitches, photo corners, etc.

clash of the hues

design discord created when cool temperature colors fight with warm temperature hues

solution

Decide if you want the overall temperature to be cool or warm. Identify the pieces that don't share this underlying hue and replace them.

neutral wash-out

a dull layout consisting of an expanse of neutral colors

solution

Add a supporting color that repeats in a few different places to spark interest through contrast.

all that jazz

a conflicting design containing bits of all the new products from the scrapbook store

solution

Pare down the accents to two pieces with common characteristics that support your theme. Use those two pieces in repetition.

static energy

such strict adherence to a symmetrical and linear structure that the layout is boring

solution

Vary the size of photos, using the strongest one for a focal point. Introduce contrasting shapes and textures to break up the strict linear quality.

sticker sneeze

sticker breeze

Supplies: Red cardstock · Patterned papers: red paisley (Anna Griffin), gold dot (K & Company), red dot (Colorbōk) · Debbie Mumm cat stickers (Creative Imaginations) · Gingham ribbon · Thread · Foam adhesive

glossary

achromatic: having no color; the use of white, black or gray

acuity: sharpness of perception

alternating rhythm: a regular pattern created by two elements alternating with one another

ambience: the total environment of a work of art as is created by the various parts of the composition working together

color temperature: the visual warmth or coolness of a color

complementary color scheme: a color grouping made up of two colors directly opposite each other on the color wheel

composition: the structural design of an artwork, consisting of the organization of the elements of design according to the principles of design

crystallographic balance: balance created by distributing elements of equal visual weight in an all-over pattern in a composition, without a point of emphasis

curvilinear: having a curving and twisting quality; reflecting the soft, flowing shape of nature (also called organic or natural)

alternating rhythm, p.108

analogous color scheme, p.60

double-complementary, p.69

analogous color scheme: a color grouping made up of colors adjacent to each other on the color wheel

asymmetrical balance: balance created on both sides of a central axis of a design when dissimilar objects have equal visual weight

balance: equal distribution of visual weight in a composition

bilateral balance: balance created when a mirror image appears on each side of the central axis of a design

color: an aspect of an object that is created by differing qualities of light reflected from it or emitted by it

color scheme: an orderly selection of colors according to logical relationships on the color wheel

concept: imagery resulting from forces within the artist, such as dreams, emotions and imagination

conceptual: having the ability to think out a general idea derived or inferred by specific criteria and put that idea into practice

continuation: a continuing line or form, such as an organic curve, a straight line or a diagonal slash, that provides unity in a design by carrying the eye through the composition

contrast: the result when opposing elements are used to produce an intensified effect in a work of art

craftsmanship: the application of skill and dexterity in creating a work of art or design

disproportionate: describing an element that, when compared to other parts in the same unit, demands either too much or not enough visual attention

double-complementary color scheme: a color grouping made up of two pairs of complementary colors, situated on the color wheel to form a square or rectangle

emphasis: to draw more attention to an area

focal point: the object of emphasis around which the rest of the design is coordinated; the center of interest, attention, and focus

form: the character and structure of the objects in a design

geometric: characterized by angular corners and contained contours, often having a man-made appearance rather than a natural one

gray scale: the progression in color values from white to black

harmony: a pleasing combination of elements within a whole

hue: the name of a color; a color in its pure form (interchangeable with the term "color")

implied line: a series of points placed in such a way that the eye automatically connects them into a line

intensity: the brightness (high intensity) or dullness (low intensity) of a color based on a hue's purity or whether gray has been added (same as chroma or saturation)

line: a series of points or a moving dot; a form that has length and very limited width

line quality: the distinguishing characteristics of the appearance of a line, contour or edge

linear: having the appearance of distinctive lines and shapes through emphasis on edges

monochromatic color scheme: a color grouping made up of different values and intensities of a single color

mood: a state of mind or emotion; a pervading impression

motif: a decorative unit

natural shape: a shape derived from anything in the natural world that is organic in appearance

focal point, p.92

negative space, p.32

proportion, p.98

negative space or shape: the secondary shape that is created in the space around a positive shape

neutral: an achromatic (white, black or gray) hue or a very low-intensity version of a hue

originality: the quality of having been created without recognizable reference to other works

organic: having a curving and twisting quality; reflecting the soft, flowing shape of nature (also called natural or curvilinear)

open space: an area left empty in a composition (also called white space)

out-of-scale: describing an element that is of a significantly different size when compared to elements of common size

pattern: created by the regular repetition of a motif in a design

photocentric: having photographs as the predominant aspect of a design

primary colors: colors that cannot be mixed from other colors; red, blue and yellow

proximity: the state of being near or next to; closeness

positive shape: the intentional, foremost forms in a design

progressive rhythm: repetition of an element that changes in increments, creating a sequential pattern

proportion: the size relationship of parts within a whole

psychic line: a mental connection between two elements that creates a visual line where there is no actual or implied line present

radial balance: balance created by elements that evenly radiate or circle out from a common central point in a design

radial composition: a design in which elements radiate from a central point

rectilinear: having a regular, precise quality; consisting of geometric shapes with angular corners

repetition: the act, process or instance of repeating or being repeated

glossary [continued]

rhythm: regular repetition of visual elements that produce the look and feel of movement and help unify a design

saturation: the vividness of a color

scale: the size of an element compared to commonly recognized objects or standard units of measurement

secondary colors: colors resulting from the mixing of two primary colors; orange, purple, and green

shade: a hue with black added; a low-value color

symmetrical balance: balance created by like shapes repeating in the same positions on either side of the central axis of a design

tactile texture: a texture that can be felt as well as seen

tertiary colors: colors resulting from mixtures of a primary and its adjacent secondary (such as red-orange and green-blue)

texture: the surface quality of an object

theme: a unifying or dominant idea; a motif

typeface: the style or design of a set of coordinating letters and/or numbers

typography: the style, arrangement and appearance of lettering

unity: the arrangement of the parts of a design into a whole; the quality of being in accord

value: the lightness (high value) or darkness (low value) of a hue

value contrast: the relationship between areas of light and dark

variety: the quality or condition of being diverse

radial balance, p.110

texture, p.43

value, p.73

shape: a visually perceived element created by either an edge, an enclosed line or by an area of color

simple rhythm: a straightforward sense of rhythm created by repetition

space: the area in which a design is created and interacts

split-complementary color scheme: a color grouping made up of three colors: one color plus the two colors on each side of its complement

sweet spot: the area in the approximate center of two abutting thirds if a design space is divided into horizontal or vertical thirds

tint: a hue with white added; a high-value color

tonality: describing the relationship of colors within a design

tone: a hue with gray or its complement added; a low-intensity color

triadic color scheme: a color grouping made up of three colors equidistant from each other on the color wheel

trompe-l'oeil: a French term meaning "fool the eye" that refers to the art of replicating the texture and value of a three-dimensional object on a flat surface so that it looks real

visual texture: a texture that is suggested to the eye but cannot be felt; an implied texture that is created by value patterns

visual triangle or quadrangle: a group of virtual points that are visually joined together to create an implied shape in a design

visual weight: the impression of how heavy or light an element appears to the eye

source guide

The following companies manufacture products featured in this book. Please check your local retailers to find these materials, or go to a company's Web site for the latest product.

100 Proof Press
(740) 594-2315
www.100proofpress.com

3L Corporation
(800) 828-3130
www.scrapbook-adhesives.com

7 Gypsies
(877) 749-7797
www.sevengypsies.com

Adobe Systems Incorporated
(866) 766-2256
www.adobe.com

American Tag Company
(800) 223-3956
www.americantag.net

American Traditional Designs®
(800) 448-6656
www.americantraditional.com

Anima Designs
(800) 570-6847
www.animadesigns.com

Anna Griffin, Inc.
(888) 817-8170
www.annagriffin.com

Art Accents, Inc.
(360) 733-8989
www.artaccents.net

ARTchix Studio
(250) 370-9985
www.artchixstudio.com

Artifacts
www.artifactsinc.com
(800) 678-4178

A Stamp In The Hand Co.
(310) 515-4818
www.astampinthehand.com

Autumn Leaves
(800) 588-6707
www.autumnleaves.com

Basic Grey™
(801) 451-6006
www.basicgrey.com

Bazzill Basics Paper
(480) 558-8557
www.bazzillbasics.com

Berwick Offray™, LLC
(800) 344-5533
www.offray.com

Be Unique
(909) 927-5357
www.beuniqueinc.com

Blue Moon Beads
(800) 377-6715
www.bluemoonbeads.com

Bo-Bunny Press
(801) 771-4010
www.bobunny.com

Boxer Scrapbook Productions
(503) 625-0455
www.boxerscrapbooks.com

Canson®, Inc.
(800) 628-9283
www.canson-us.com

Carolee's Creations®
(435) 563-1100
www.ccpaper.com

Cavallini Papers & Co., Inc.
(800) 226-5287
www.cavallini.com

Chatterbox, Inc.
(208) 939-9133
www.chatterboxinc.com

Chronicle Books
(800) 722-6656
www.chroniclebooks.com

Clearsnap, Inc.
(360) 293-6634
www.clearsnap.com

Club Scrap™, Inc.
(888) 634-9100
www.clubscrap.com

Colorbök™, Inc.
(800) 366-4660
www.colorbok.com

Colors by Design
(800) 832-8436
www.colorsbydesign.com

Craft Cut
no contact info

Creative Imaginations
(800) 942-6487
www.cigift.com

Creative Impressions Rubber Stamps, Inc.
(719) 596-4860
www.creativeimpressions.com

Creek Bank Creations, Inc.
(217) 427-5980
www.creekbankcreations.com

Cross-My Heart-Cards, Inc.
(888) 689-8808
www.crossmyheart.com

C-Thru® Ruler Company, The
(800) 243-8419
www.cthruruler.com

Daisy D's Paper Company
(888) 601-8955
www.daisydspaper.com

Delta Technical Coatings, Inc.
(800) 423-4135
www.deltacrafts.com

Deluxe Designs
(480) 497-9005
www.deluxedesigns.com

DeNami Design Rubber Stamps
(253) 437-1626
www.denamidesign.com

Design Originals
(800) 877-0067
www.d-originals.com

Die Cuts With A View
(801) 224-6766
www.diecutswithaview.com

DMD Industries, Inc.
(800) 805-9890
www.dmdind.com

Doodlebug Design™ Inc.
(801) 966-9952
www.doodlebug.ws

Dove of the East
www.doveoftheeast.com

Dymo
(800) 426-7827
www.dymo.com

EK Success™, Ltd.
(800) 524-1349
www.eksuccess.com

Emagination Crafts, Inc.
(866) 238-9770
www.emaginationcrafts.com

Epson America, Inc.
(562) 981-3840
www.epson.com

Family Treasures®
(949) 290-0872
www.familytreasures.com

FiberMark
(802) 257-0365
http://scrapbook.fibermark.com

Fiskars®, Inc.
(800) 950-0203
www.fiskars.com

Flair® Designs
(888) 546-9990
www.flairdesignsinc.com

FoofaLa
(402) 330-3208
www.foofala.com

Frances Meyer, Inc.®
(413) 584-5446
www.francesmeyer.com

Grafix®
(800) 447-2349
www.grafix.com

Green Pear Studio
www.greenpear.com

Hambly Studios, Inc.
(800) 451-3399
www.hamblystudios.com

Hampton Art Stamps, Inc.
(800) 229-1019
www.hamptonart.com

Heart & Home, Inc.
(905) 686-9031
www.heartandhome.com

Heidi Swapp/Advantus Corporation
(904) 482-0092
www.heidiswapp.com

Hero Arts® Rubber Stamps, Inc.
(800) 822-4376
www.heroarts.com

Hot Off The Press, Inc.
(800) 227-9595
www.b2b.hotp.com
www.paperpizazz.com

Inkadinkado® Rubber Stamps
(800) 888-4652
www.inkadinkado.com

JHB International
(303) 751-8100
www.buttons.com

JudiKins
(310) 515-1115
www.judikins.com

Junkitz™
(732) 792-1108
www.junkitz.com

Just For Fun® Rubber Stamps
(727) 938-9898
www.jffstamps.com

K & Company
(888) 244-2083
www.kandcompany.com

Kangaroo & Joey®, Inc.
(800) 646-8065
www.kangarooandjoey.com

Karen Combs
www.karencombs.com

Karen Foster Design
(801) 451-9779
www.karenfosterdesign.com

Keeping Memories Alive™
(800) 419-4949
www.scrapbooks.com

KI Memories
(972) 243-5595
www.kimemories.com

Kodomo, Inc.
(650) 685-1828
www.kodomoinc.com

Kolo® LLC
(888) 636-5656
www.kolo.com

Krylon®
(216) 566-200
www.krylon.com

Li'l Davis Designs
(949) 838-0344
www.lildavisdesigns.com

LuminArte
(formerly Angelwing Enterprises)
(866) 229-1544
www.luminarteinc.com

Magenta Rubber Stamps
(800) 565-5254
www.magentastyle.com

Magic Mesh
(651) 345-6374
www.magicmesh.com

Magic Scraps™
(972) 238-1838
www.magicscraps.com

Making Memories
(800) 286-5263
www.makingmemories.com

Mara-Mi, Inc.
(800) 627-2648
www.mara-mi.com

Marcel Schurman
(800) 333-6724
www.schurmanfinepapers.com

Mark Enterprises
see Stampendous!

Maruca Designs
www.marucadesigns.com

**Marvy® Uchida/
Uchida of America, Corp.**
(800) 541-5877
www.uchida.com

May Arts
(800) 442-3950
www.mayarts.com

**Mayco® (a division of
Coloramics, LLC)**
(614) 876-1171
www.maycocolors.com

me & my BiG ideas®
(949) 883-2065
www.meandmybigideas.com

Memories Complete™, LLC
(866) 966-6365
www.memoriescomplete.com

Meri Meri
www.merimeri.com

Michaels® Arts & Crafts
(800) 642-4235
www.michaels.com

MOD-my own design
(303) 641-8680
www.mod-myowndesign.com

Moda Fabrics/United Notions
(800) 527-9447
www.unitednotions.com

Moote Points
www.mootepoints.com

Mrs. Grossman's Paper Company
(800) 429-4549
www.mrsgrossmans.com

My Mind's Eye™, Inc.
(800) 665-5116
www.frame-ups.com

Nature's Pressed
(800) 850-2499
www.naturespressed.com

NRN Designs
(800) 421-6958
www.nrndesigns.com

Nunn Design
(360) 379-3557
www.nunndesign.com

Offray
see Berwick Offray, LLC

Paper Adventures®
(973) 406-5000
www.paperadventures.com

Paper Company, The/ANW Crestwood
(800) 525-3196
www.anwcrestwood.com

Paper Fever, Inc.
(800) 477-0902
www.paperfever.com

Paper House Productions®
(800) 255-7316
www.paperhouseproductions.com

Paula Best & Co.
(831) 632-0587
www.paulabest.com

Picture Show
PO Box 65440
St. Paul, MN 55165

Plaid Enterprises, Inc.
(800) 842-4197
www.plaidonline.com

Prima Marketing, Inc.
(909) 627-5532
www.mulberrypaperflowers.com

PrintWorks
(800) 854-6558
www.printworkscollection.com

Prism™ Papers
(866) 902-1002
www.prismpapers.com

Provo Craft®
(888) 577-3545
www.provocraft.com

Prym-Dritz
www.dritz.com

Ranger Industries, Inc.
(800) 244-2211
www.rangerink.com

Renaissance Ribbons
(877) 422-6601
www.renaissanceribbons.com

Rubba Dub Dub
(707) 748-0929
www.artsanctum.com

Rubber Baby Buggy Bumpers
see Stamp Francisco

Rubberstamp Ave.
(541) 665-9981
www.rubberstampave.com

Rubber Stampede
(800) 423-4135
www.deltacrafts.com

Rubber Stamps of America
(800) 553-5031
www.stampusa.com

Rusty Pickle
(801) 746-1045
www.rustypickle.com

Sakura Hobby Craft
(310) 212-7878
www.sakuracraft.com

Sandylion Sticker Designs
(800) 387-4215
www.sandylion.com

Savvy Stamps
(866) 44-SAVVY
www.savvystamps.com

ScrapArts
(503) 631-4893
www.scraparts.com

Scrapbook Wizard™, The
(435) 752-7555
www.scrapbookwizard.com

Scrapworks, LLC
(801) 363-1010
www.scrapworks.com

Scrapyard 329
(775) 829-1118
www.scrapyard329.com

Staedtler®, Inc.
(800) 927-7723
www.staedtler.us

Stamp A Mania
(505) 524-7099
www.stampamania.com

Stamp Francisco
www.stampfrancisco.com
(360) 210-4031

Stampa Rosa
no longer in business

Stampabilities®
(800) 888-0321
www.stampabilities.com

Stampendous!®
(800) 869-0474
www.stampendous.com

Stampin' Up!®
(800) 782-6787
www.stampinup.com

Stampington & Company
(877) STAMPER
www.stampington.com

Stamps by Judith
www.stampsbyjudith.com

Stamps Happen, Inc.®
(714) 879-9894
www.stampshappen.com

Sulky® of America
(800) 874-4115
www.sulky.com

Sulyn Industries, Inc.
(800) 257-8596
www.sulyn.com

Technique Tuesday, LLC
(503) 644-4073
www.techniquetuesday.com

Therm O Web, Inc.
(800) 323-0799
www.thermoweb.com

Treehouse Designs
(501) 372-1109
www.treehouse-designs.com

Tsukineko®, Inc.
(800) 769-6633
www.tsukineko.com

USArtQuest, Inc.
(517) 522-6225
www.usartquest.com

Vintage Workshop® LLC, The
(913) 341-5559
www.thevintageworkshop.com

Wimpole Street Creations
(801) 298-0504
www.wimpolestreet.com

Wordsworth
(719) 282-3495
www.wordsworthstamps.com

index

Learn more about scrapbooking great layouts with these other fine books from Memory Makers!

Ask the Masters!
ISBN-10: 1-892127-88-1
ISBN-13: 978-1-892127-88-4
Z0277

Scrapbooker's Essential Guide to Color
ISBN-10: 1-892127-80-6
ISBN-13: 978-1-892127-80-8
Z0020

What About the Words?
ISBN-10: 1-892127-77-6
ISBN-13: 978-1-892127-77-8
Z0017

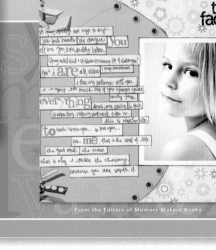